Aquarobics

Aquarobics

Getting fit and keeping fit in the swimming pool

Glenda Baum

MCSP, SRP

LONDON · BOSTON

First published in 1987
by Faber and Faber Limited
3 Queen Square, London WC1N 3AU

Photoset and printed in Great Britain by
Redwood Burn Limited, Trowbridge, Wiltshire

British Library Cataloguing in Publication Data

Baum, Glenda
Aquarobics.
1. Aquatic exercises 2. Physical fitness
I. Title
613.7'1 RA781.17

ISBN 0–571–14746–1

For my husband, Harold
the flexible mind in the inflexible body!

Contents

Acknowledgements

If I had never come across Jenny Forrest, and her pool, where music is on tap(e), I should not have developed Aquarobics, and there would have been no book. Without the help, support and grammatical guidance of my husband, Harold, there would also have been no book.

To move from the negative to the positive: I should like to thank the hundreds of patients for getting better with the help of Aquarobics, and for their encouragement to me to take up the pen and put down the flipper!

On a more practical level, I should like to thank my various physiotherapy colleagues whom I have bored with sections of this book. To name but a few, Jenny Brown, Chris van Langenberghe, Margie Polden, Harvinder Panesar. I am also grateful to Mark Saunders for his update on exercise physiology.

On a much more mundane level, I should like to thank the back-up 'team' of Fenella, Bobbie, Enid and Anne for services rendered, from constant coffee to coping with the phone calls. I hope that this book will be sufficiently successful for me to have to thank my accountant David Berke!

For the illustrations, I should like to thank Katy Staton who skilfully and efficiently sketched my frantic movements into a form for Audrey Besterman to turn them into such splendid drawings.

I should like to thank my son David for initiating me into the art of the word processor – which eased the chore of writing, and Amstrad (and Kall-Kwik photocopying) for

helping me carry on after I had wiped my master disc clean.
I must thank my nearest and dearest (my parents, my husband and my three offspring, David, Mandy and Alison) for all the additional washing-up that no doubt they had to do, and apologise to them for my bad temper.

1

Why Aquarobics?

Life started in the water: the very first movements a baby performs are reflex 'kicks' in amniotic fluid, within its mother's womb. It is no accident that babies enjoy their bath-time – they are in their original environment. Swimming, for survival, is instinctive for most mammals, and quite a few land animals 'play' in the water for pleasure. Through the ages, man has used bodies of water, not just as places to carry out his laundry and his ablutions, but to meet friends, exchange news and enjoy life a little. Originally these were natural geographic sites such as rivers, lakes or the sea-shore, but as civilisation progressed so water was artificially collected, and sometimes even heated, in such structures as Roman baths.

Immersion in water has been used for therapy since time immemorial. There are also various ways in which treatment can be performed 'around' water. Hot mud packs may be applied to various parts of the body, massage may be given using jets of water – these latter being more widely practised on the European mainland. The most effective therapeutic way in which water is used, however, is as a medium in which to exercise. In the United Kingdom (UK), physiotherapists have been treating patients by hydrotherapy for as long as there have been physiotherapists. Traditionally these pools were heated to higher temperatures, usually above 36°C.

Some three years ago I had built a hydrotherapy pool. Its design was quite modest, but I subsequently realised that it was unique in this country in physiotherapy. The special features of this pool are that music can be played, that there is a facility to make an extremely strong current of water against which one can exercise, and that the water temperature is tepid rather than warm or hot. There is also a separate hot-water spa bath (Jacuzzi), which is very pleasant, and hence very relaxing. Working with patients, using this combined facility, on a day-to-day basis, I almost unintentionally developed a series of simple exercises for various conditions and various parts of the body. These can be performed effectively (but in different ways) by people of such a wide range of ability and age as recovering athletes, 80-year-olds with degenerative neurological or orthopaedic conditions, and patients with problems in their backs, shoulders, hips, knees, ankles, and a lot of bits in between! The same exercises are also useful as a keep-fit programme. Most of them can be performed in an ordinary swimming-pool, and this is precisely what I try to encourage my patients to do.

There has been a rapid increase in the number of public as well as private swimming-pools in recent years. This is because the general public is now much more health and fitness orientated, and swimming is thought by many to be the perfect form of exercise. Many public pools are run at a higher temperature than they used to be. Many have specific times set aside when it is possible to exercise without hordes of young children splashing around. My hope is that the day will come when public pools will set aside a certain time every day for 'exercise', rather than merely swimming, in the shallow end of the pool: appropriate music will be played over the public-address system, and the young and the old, the fit and the not-so-fit will be able to exercise together.

Physiologically, there are many advantages that exercising in water has over exercising on dry land. Water counteracts the effect of gravity: in other words, one is weightless in water. When standing in shoulder-deep water, there is no weight going through the spine, hips, knees or feet.

Normally the downward force of gravity means that

weight-bearing joint surfaces, such as those just mentioned, are compressed into each other. It means that the intervertebral discs (the washer-like structures found between the bones of the spine) are under compression. The buoyancy of water is an upward acting force, however, so instead of the joints being wedged together, in water they are tending to be floated apart. If a joint is damaged in some way, it may well be painful to move it when the structures are pressed together, i.e. if weight is going through it. If, though, the bony ends are not jarred together as movement takes place, then the movement may well not be painful or harmful.

The function of joints is to move; hence, to be able to move normally without causing pain is therapeutic to a damaged joint. Moreover, there is a physiological sequence in the body which can be simplified as: movement causes pain, pain makes muscles get weak, weak muscles allow the joints to be injured further, this causes more pain, more stiffness, thus causing further weakness . . . and so on. This vicious circle of pain, weakness, stiffness is, alas, only too well known to all members of the caring professions. If there were some way of carrying out normal movement without pain, then the vicious circle would be transformed into a beneficial one: movement leading to improvement of functioning of joints and muscles, leading to stronger muscles and better quality of movement, and to a restoration of normality. Exercising in water often allows this to happen. But it is necessary to issue a warning at this point: in order to get on to the beneficial circle, and not on to the harmful one, one should never exercise *through* pain. If a movement is made *up to*, but not through the pain, the pain should subside. By continuing very gently, the size of the movement should increase, and the ache subside. If, however, the pain continues or gets worse, then that particular movement must be stopped. Doing the prescribed exercises in water should be helpful, and not harmful, as long as that basic principle is observed.

It is also necessary to state at this point that allowing the body to move normally, perhaps for the first time in a while, is quite powerful medicine. Any medicine is dangerous in excess, and so care must be taken not to have an overdose of exercise – especially in the early stages.

In a way, one can describe the buoyancy effect of water as being a mechanical aid to movement, but it is not that simple. Water can act to 'assist' certain movements, or it can be used to make movements a bit harder. An example of the former would be that if one stands in shoulder-high water, then both arms will float to the surface – assuming the arm and shoulder muscles are relaxed. Sometimes it is impossible to bring the arms up to an equivalent position on dry land because the shoulder muscles may be too weak or damaged to lift the arms up against the weight of gravity, or the joints may be too painful when the muscles are working.

Water is 1000 times more dense than air. Therefore if one does a quick movement, such as straightening the knee when standing on the other leg, which is very easy out of the water, it can be quite hard work when done in water, assuming the limb is arranged in such a way as to 'push' the water out of the way. The more 'drag' in the water, the harder the muscles have to work. It is therefore possible to use exercise in water to make muscles work harder than they would have done to perform the same movement out of water, and this speeds up the strengthening process.

There is one other major reason why exercising in water can be very helpful, and that is to help with balance and co-ordination. However, in order for this to happen, one must treat the water as though it is not there! In other words, one must try to remain 'in balance' (i.e. the centre of gravity of the body should remain over the feet). One of the good things about getting into water is that one can lie around in funny positions, and have the security of knowing that it does not matter if one 'falls over' as there is nowhere to fall to! This only applies if the person in the water is not afraid of drowning. So it is better if the exerciser is able to swim and does not mind getting his face wet. Despite that, none of the exercises calls for immersion of the head, but to get maximum benefit from them, one should be relaxed, and positively enjoying the sensation that the three-dimensional support of water gives. Indeed, enjoyment is a crucial factor in the system, because if the mind is happy and reassured, then the body can start to get better. I have had success with many people who think they hate the water, or cannot swim, but it requires a one-to-one supervision until they have got their confidence. If the water is too cold, or is unpleasant to get into, then it will spoil the enjoyment, and hence the therapeutic benefits. One may have to gear the exercises so as to engender warmth, and perhaps stay in for a shorter time.

How then can exercising in water help balance and co-ordination? It is necessary to understand a little of how the body's sensory system works. Everybody knows that muscles cause movements by contracting, but how does the muscle know where and how much to move? For an apparently simple movement, like waving to somebody, the 'electronics' within the body are staggering. It is not just a question of waving a hand up and down at the wrist joint. All the other muscles in that arm require action to stabilise them in whatever position is wanted. For every muscle that 'contracts', the one on the opposite side has to be programmed to 'let go' or be passively 'played out' (like a fishing-line). The easiest example of this is in the upper arm, as the muscle system there is simpler for demonstration purposes than in other parts of the body. Basically, there is the biceps, which bends the elbow when it contracts, and the triceps, which straightens the arm when it contracts. However, in order to bend the elbow, the triceps must allow itself to be played out so that it can lengthen (Fig. 1/1).

To wave the hand, then, all the 46 muscles in one upper

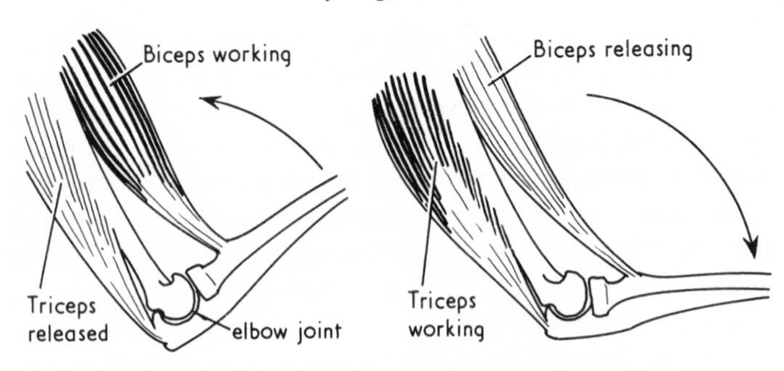

Fig. 1/1 The mechanism of muscle action

arm need to have messages sent to them, and in return send information back to the brain, so as to monitor the movement in order for it to be a smooth co-ordinated one. And if that were not enough, raising one's arm alters the centre of gravity, and so messages to monitor this must come from the millions of nerve-endings in all the joints and muscles and skin. The information is then immediately processed and monitored so that appropriate muscle action can be taken so that you do not fall over.

You can see that normal movement involves an extremely complicated monitoring and instruction system of messages going from the sensory receptors (i.e. the movement-monitoring receptors in the skin, joints and muscles; the visual messages coming in from the eyes and the orientation-sensing labyrinth in the inner ear), and going back to instruct muscles. When this monitoring/instruction system goes wrong, then movement is jerky or unco-ordinated, balance is bad, or there may even be a paralysis. There is often nothing wrong with the muscles or joints, but there is with the wiring or circuit pathways. The medical term for this type of condition is a 'neurological disorder'.

Unfortunately, as part of the ageing process, the 'wiring' tends to deteriorate a bit and the joints to degenerate. The brain, though, has an amazing capacity for finding an

Fig. 1/2 Righting reflex. To avoid falling over, the arm and leg lift

alternative neurological (electrical) pathway even when it has been badly damaged. To 'programme' the brain, one has to go through the motions of, for example, getting off balance and then correcting this. The trouble is that to do this on dry land, there is a real danger of falling over and hurting oneself, whereas in water all movements are slowed down, thus giving time to do the correction before falling over.

There are two basic balance mechanisms. The first is to counteract the loss of balance (which is when the centre of gravity is not over the base) by moving in such a way as to bring the centre of gravity over the feet again. An example of this is, if falling to the right, there is a reflex that lifts up the left arm, so as to shift the centre of gravity of the body to the left (Fig. 1/2). These are the important 'righting reflexes' that are developed in childhood and are needed to keep us in whatever position we wish to remain, counteracting forces of gravity, responding to being tripped up, or pushed over.

The other reflex is a 'fail-safe' when the first one no longer works. It is the reflex to put out your hands to catch yourself – to avoid hitting your head you land on your hands instead, or grab hold of something. It often happens in neurological conditions, or in old age, that the 'grab–hold' reflex is stronger than the 'righting reflex'. This can be hazardous because you often grab things that are not meant to be grabbed, so you still end up on the floor! But the righting reflexes can be re-educated, to a certain extent, and water is an ideal medium in which to do this. This gives rise to the third basic principle of Aquarobics, which is to use the water as though it is not there. In other words, to be in balance all the time. Some of the exercises tend to put one off balance, but practice makes perfect, as by practising one is re-programming the nerve pathways, as already described.

2

The Principles of Aquarobics

1. Do not push through pain.
2. Movements should look normal.
3. Use the water as though it were not there (remain in balance).
4. Moderation and sensible progression.

DO NOT PUSH THROUGH PAIN

Pain is usually there for a reason, and it can be dangerous to ignore it. When in the water, however, if movement is slow and gentle, it is almost impossible to harm oneself without it hurting. So if one can carry out normal body movements as long as it does not hurt, then it should be helpful. Do not take pain-killers (analgesics) before going into the water, or it might be possible to 'push through' the pain without realising it.

Pain that is coming from muscles and joints is worse at the extremes of the range and less in the middle (Fig. 2/1).

Therefore, if one starts moving in the middle of the range, it should not hurt, but it may begin to hurt either as one bends or straightens. As long as any movement is initially performed slowly and gently then it is possible to 'just nudge' the pain. In other words, at the first sign of a pain, stop the movement and reverse the direction. *Never keep moving with the pain getting worse as you do*. However, if you 'just nudge' the pain, and repeat the movement to the same point, you may well find that next time there is not even a 'nudge' – in other

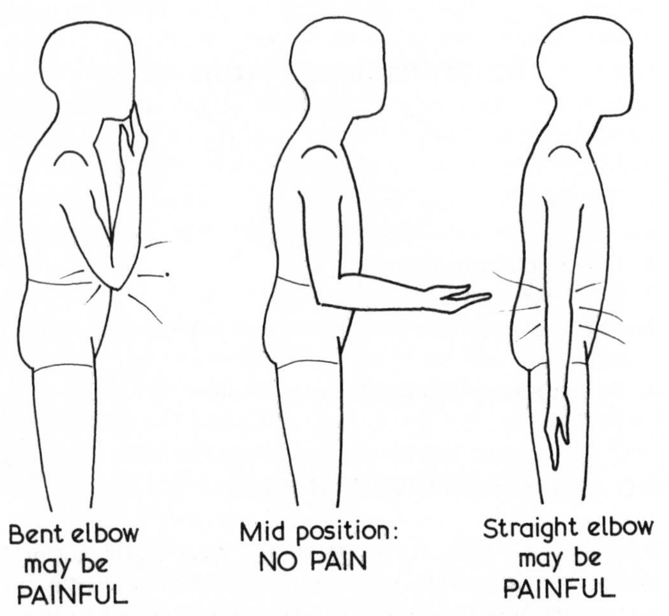

Fig. 2/1 Relationship of pain to joint position

words, it is usually the case that if a movement is repeated, without 'nudging' each time, then the pain gets less, and so the range of the movement can be bigger. This is a good thing to do, and is a principle behind Aquarobics. If, however, when repeating the movement it gets worse instead of better, then you *must stop*, and try something else. If three consecutive exercises have to be stopped then get out of the water.

MOVEMENTS SHOULD LOOK NORMAL

The more one knows about anatomy, the more one realises the miraculous complexity of the human body. Every part has its purpose and the interconnections and ramifications are indeed mind-boggling. The basic purpose of the musculo-skeletal system is to allow movement to take place. We are used to looking at machines, and are all familiar with the concept of 'servicing', 'repair' and 'wearing-out'. To some extent the same applies with the body. A well 'maintained' body is less likely to wear out. Similarly, an over- or inappropriately-used body is more likely to wear out. Joints are there to be moved, and muscles are there to bring about the movement, and all of our joints and muscles should be put through a full-range movement every day or so. However, I do not think that the average body was designed to take the pounding of long-distance running. Although the legs and heart are being exercised, the spine, hips and knees must be getting worn out because of the body-weight compressing them with every step. That is why non-weight-bearing exercise in water is so very helpful, as it does not facilitate the degenerative syndrome.

We are designed to move, and if we do not move we atrophy (waste). But our movements should be physiologically normal ones. They should look good – graceful, never awkward. The brain does not know individual muscles, it only works in terms of movements. Sometimes if a joint is stuck, then in order to make the required movement, other near-by joints are made to play 'tricks'. It may be necessary to allow this to happen in order to cope with the day-to-day problems of living, but not, please, in the water (if at all avoidable).

The very fact of performing the 'odd' movement is reconditioning the brain, and other muscles and joints, that it is a normal movement. Usually the abnormal movement happens at the extremes of the range. If that is the case, then it is better to perform a small normal movement than a large abnormal one.

The exception to this is that there are certain medical conditions where normal movement is impossible. For example, if a nerve is damaged then a muscle, or a group of muscles, may be paralysed. There may have been damage or disease to the central nervous system, for example after having a stroke, or in the case of multiple sclerosis or Parkinson's disease. In those cases it may be impossible to make normal movements, but water should make it easier to move as it slows everything down. In such cases, the Aquarobic exercises should be done to look as normal as possible. Thus one re-programmes the brain towards normality.

USE THE WATER AS THOUGH IT WERE NOT THERE

This principle follows on from the previous one. The whole concept of Aquarobics is to pattern the body to fitness and health by doing normal movements in water. One hopes to get a 'carry-over' effect. The aim of doing walking exercises in the pool is to improve the quality of normal walking. It is easy when in water to lean about at all kinds of peculiar angles without falling over and hurting oneself. Fun though this may be, it does not help to regain normal dry-land function (Fig. 2/2). Those exercises which are performed standing up should be done standing straight and square. To disregard this principle encourages bad movement patterns.

MODERATION AND SENSIBLE PROGRESSION

I am an ardent believer in 'the middle of the road' for most situations in life – except driving. The problem with extremes is that there is often an easy swing to the opposite extreme. One has only to look at a pendulum to illustrate this – pull the weight a long way over to one side and it will swing way over to the other side. If, though, the weight is allowed to rock

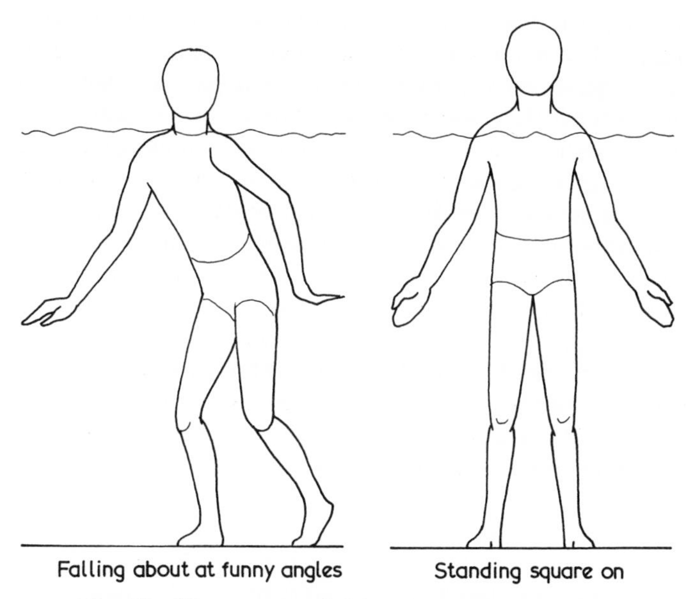

Fig. 2/2 The wrong and right way of using the water

gently near the middle, then it will stay there. One of the reasons that I am against some of the more extreme dry-land forms of exercise (such as aerobics) is that human nature makes one's initial enthusiasm wane, and there is then a temptation to give up all forms of exercise. It is the old story of the tortoise and the hare – sensible moderation and perseverance get there in the end. I believe in a sensible middle-of-the-road life style – that some exercise is a necessity – but that an excess of anything is bad for you. It is considered beneficial to work the heart to the point where you get breathless, and this is certainly possible in the pool, but I do not recommend exercising to the point of exhaustion – that is counter-productive.

Muscles only get stronger if they are worked to the 'point of fatigue'. But that does not mean that the whole body has to be fatigued – it means only that that particular muscle should be tired. However, as the same muscle gets stronger, over days and weeks, then the 'point of fatigue' moves farther on. Therefore any exercising that is aiming to strengthen muscle should be progressive. In other words, on the subsequent exercise session, one should either repeat the same exercise a few more times, or move more quickly through the water, or modify the exercise. Not all of the exercises should be advanced, however, but the overall schedule for the day should be a little harder than the previous session. This is the basic principle behind rehabilitation and is crucial to returning to former fitness. There are, alas, cases where this is not possible. If one is fighting a slowly progressive disability, then to remain 'static' is a great achievement.

3
Warnings

I have supervised Aquarobics with people aged from 14 to 85 (who between them have had a complete spectrum of disabilities), without any complications. Nevertheless, I do advise that if you have *any* kind of physical problem (rather than just wanting to do Aquarobics to keep fit), you should consult your medical adviser first, and get his/her approval.

If, having obtained medical approval, you decide to 'take the plunge', it is necessary to be cautious. Ill people will find the hassle of going to a public swimming-pool very tiring. It is difficult to cope with crowds, noise, and getting dressed and undressed in a hot, humid atmosphere.

In my physiotherapy practice, all patients are required to rest for a minimum of 30 minutes, after exercising in the water. Whereas that is standard practice at a hydrotherapy pool, it may not be so easy to arrange at a public pool. There is often, though, a resting area, and perhaps even a cafeteria where a drink may be obtained and slowly drunk.

If you have, or have recently had, a breathing problem, then you *must* check with your doctor before going to the pool. The pressure of the water on your chest wall can make it much harder to breathe, and could be dangerous. You should not go near a pool if you have chronic serious respiratory disease, or if you are recovering from a chest infection, especially pneumonia. Asthmatics, on the other hand, may obtain positive benefit from Aquarobics or swimming.

People who are generally in good health, but are suffering

temporarily from the odd backache, pain in the knee, etc., should find no problem, but it is advisable to make the first session shorter – just to give the body time to adapt. The motto must be 'Moderation and Common Sense'.

If somebody is accustomed to taking exercise and is fit, then there should be no problem in coping with a half-hour session, but do make it a gentle session the first time. The speed and strength can always be built up at subsequent sessions in a sensible and logical way.

If, however, you are recovering from an illness, or a recent infection, then it is obviously better to err on the side of caution. Do not attempt Aquarobics if you have had a raised temperature within the previous 48 hours.

Skin infections, bacterial or fungal, or incontinence of faeces are incompatible with Aquarobics. However, a very minor degree of stress incontinence (a small leakage of urine on coughing) may be acceptable. Ask the person in charge of the pool.

Aquarobics are especially helpful following fractures of the legs, or orthopaedic surgery. Do check first with your doctor. If you are not allowed to take weight through the bad leg, you will be able to walk in chest-high water, as you are virtually weightless in the water. But remember that if the water is shallower than that, then some weight will be going through the damaged limb, so be particularly careful getting into and out of a public pool. It may not be possible to get in (if, for example, there is only a ladder) if you are not allowed to take weight through a leg. Some pools have difficult arrangements for getting in and out of the water, and the changing facilities and clothes storage procedures may be awkward. These will all have to be investigated to ensure that you can cope. Sometimes public pools allot a special time for people with special difficulties, when the general public is excluded. It is worth while enquiring to see if this facility is available at your local pool.

For those lucky people with their own pools or with amenable friends who have suitable ones – then good luck and enjoy yourselves!

4

Music and Rhythm

Appropriate music is really essential to successful Aquarobics. The exercises do not have the same impact when performed without music. It may be you have to make your own music, by singing to yourself. In my physiotherapy practice, there is an immediate onset of lethargy if the tape runs out. Anybody who has done dry-land exercise classes will appreciate how the music plays an integral part of the proceedings.

All societies, from primitive tribes to the ultra-sophisticated, incorporate music and dance into their customs. Indeed, moving rhythmically to music is surely the most primitive of all pleasures. Anthropologists have, no doubt, many explanations about why this is helpful to the community as a whole. Dancing is certainly enjoyable and pleasurable to the individual.

In my physiotherapy practice I have discovered a few cassettes that are particularly suitable for use with my exercise programmes. The essential characteristics are that the music must have a strong 'beat', preferably in a moderate-to-fast tempo with the occasional slower track; and no vocal because I have found that to be distracting. I have about six cassettes which I use regularly. I select the livelier ones for the younger or fitter patients, and vice versa.

Ideally, the cassette should last 30 minutes a side, as that is the usual exercise time. Shorter cassettes create the problem of how to turn them over without dripping water on to an electrical appliance. It is possible to combine two shorter tapes on to one longer one by re-recording.

The following is a list of the cassettes that I regularly use.

This list is an example rather than a set of definitive recommendations. It has arisen rather arbitrarily and not as a result of a scientific survey of what is available.

1. 'The Best of Hooked on Classics', by the Royal Philharmonic Orchestra. There are several in this series, all of which are musically suitable, but some of them last only 15 minutes.
2. 'Digital Ragtime', with Joshua Rifkin on the piano.
3. 'Red Hot and Ragtime', featuring the music of Scott Joplin and Jelly Roll Morton.
4. 'Rondo Veneziano – Venice in Peril'. There are several other similar ones – suitable if you like them, but all short.
5. 'Music from the Greek Islands'. Not everybody's taste, but sometimes useful, especially for the walking exercises. It is challenging at times as one or two of the tracks get quicker and quicker!
6. Ballet music such as Meyerbeer's 'Les Patineurs' with Massenet's 'Le Cid' on the reverse side (Decca KSXC 6812). Almost all ballet music is suitable for Aquarobics, but the men may not feel comfortable using it.

Pop music may well be suitable and indeed, preferable to the younger Aquarobic fan, but I am sorry to say that I am unable to recommend any particular cassettes!

It helps if you know the music really well, then you can time the number of your exercises to fit in, so that you have allowed just enough time to work both limbs. You will find that subsequent sessions will be more enjoyable, as they give an opportunity to choreograph your exercises as you get to know your music better. If the music is good and you like it, then each time will be better than the previous one.

For those lucky people with their own swimming-pools, music will not present a problem. It is hoped that if this book becomes successful, then public pools will have suitable music playing over their public address systems. In the meantime, if you are exercising in a public pool then there are two options only available to you. One is to sing (albeit silently) some easy rhythmic tune like 'John Brown's Body' or 'She'll be coming round the mountain when she comes'. It does not really matter what you sing inside your head as long as it is rhythmic and you can keep it going for 30 minutes.

The other option is to use one of the splashproof cassette players that can be bought. It may be difficult to leave it at the side of the pool, in case it gets knocked in or stolen. They are not designed for immersion, and therefore cannot be used hanging from your neck, but they can be placed on your head in a suitable splashproof hat which you can either make yourself or, hopefully, purchase.

5

The Exercises

Exercises 1 to 32 are performed in the upright position. Unless otherwise stated, stand in water that is between chest and waist deep. Have the feet slightly apart to help balance. Exercises 33 to 40 are performed lying, that is floating, on the water.

EXERCISES 1 TO 15 (FOR THE TRUNK AND LEGS)

Exercise 1 'Changes' (Fig. 5/1)

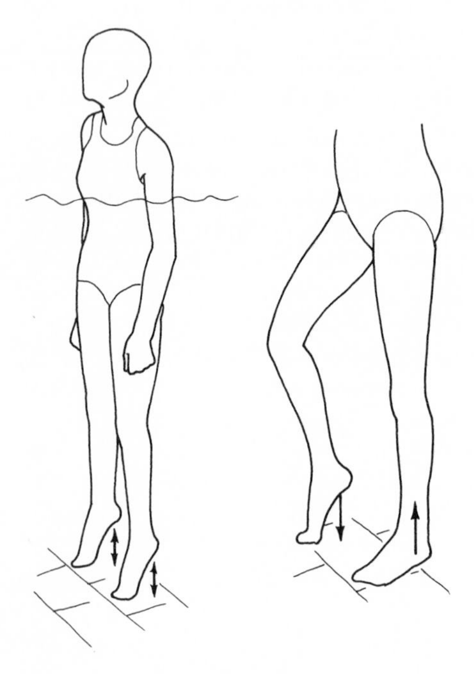

5/1

REASONS FOR DOING IT

To give one confidence to move around in the water.
To mobilise the ankles, toes and knees.
To restore the bounce to walking!
To get warm, useful if the water is cold.
To give encouragement, as many people can do this in the water, but not on dry land.

To get a little breathless, and so work the cardiovascular system.

HOW TO DO IT

Starting position: Stand with the feet just a little apart. Hold on if necessary.

Move: To begin with, go up and down on your toes, so that both feet bend at the big toe joints, but the knees are straight.

When you are comfortable doing that without feeling that you are falling over, then transfer your weight from one foot to the other, by peeling one heel off the floor of the pool (with the other foot flat), but leaving the tip of the big toe in contact with the floor of the pool. As each heel rises in turn, so the knee of the leg that is lifting up will bend forward. Throughout this sequence you will need to imagine that the end of each big toe is stuck to the floor of the pool.

Finally, continue pumping the weight from one big toe to the other, but getting a feeling of bounce as you do it. The head should bob up and down with each step. This is a stationary exercise.

Exercise 2 Leg swinging (Fig. 5/2)

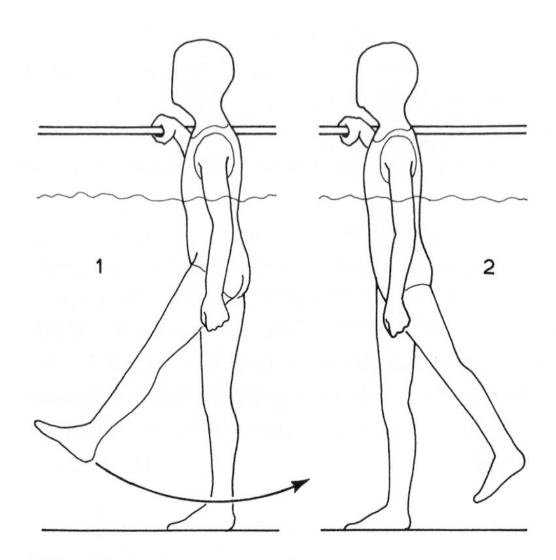

5/2

REASONS FOR DOING IT

Do it slowly and gently to loosen up the joints of the hips and lower back.
Do it more quickly to strengthen the muscles in the back, buttock and the thighs.
Do it very slowly, without holding on, to improve balance.

HOW TO DO IT

Starting position: Hold on to the side with one hand, with the body facing at right angles to the wall. Stand, in balance, on the leg nearer the wall.
Move: Brace all the muscles in the other leg, and keeping the knee absolutely straight, swing the stiff leg slowly and *gently*

backwards and forwards, while keeping the rest of the body still, and straight. Keep the toes and ankle pulled up, or you will stub your big toe on the floor of the pool. The standing foot should be flat on the floor of the pool. Reverse (i.e. face the other way and hold on with the other hand), and repeat with the other leg*. Many of us have a secret hankering to be able to move like a ballet dancer. This 'barre' exercise is the nearest we shall get to it, so make the most of it!

CAUTION

Start this exercise very slowly and gently to see whether it causes any pain. Remember, if it does, only barely 'nudge' the pain, then reverse the direction of movement (see Fig. 1/1, p. 6). Remember the basic principle: *Do not push through pain*.

* Remember, only the leg should move. The head and hips should keep perfectly still.

Exercise 3 Sideways leg swinging (Fig. 5/3)

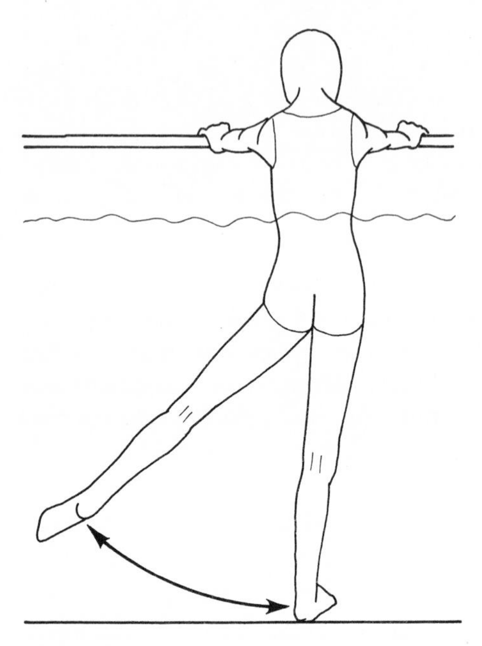

5/3

REASONS FOR DOING IT

To mobilise the joints of the hips, pelvis and lower spine, if done slowly using alternate legs.

To work the muscles in the backside, the hips and inner thighs, if done more quickly with alternate legs or the same leg repeated.

To strengthen these same muscles, if it is done with one leg and repeated very quickly.

To help improve balance, if it is done without holding on. In this case, if necessary, rest one finger on the side of the pool, but try not to hold on. Use alternate legs.

HOW TO DO IT

Starting position: Face the side of the pool and hold on with both hands. Stand on one leg (keeping that heel down).

Move: Slowly lift the other leg out to the side, and put it down. Keep the trunk still, only the one leg should move at a time. Repeat either with alternate legs, or with the same leg, depending on the reason for doing the exercise.

Exercise 4 Corkscrew (Fig. 5/4)

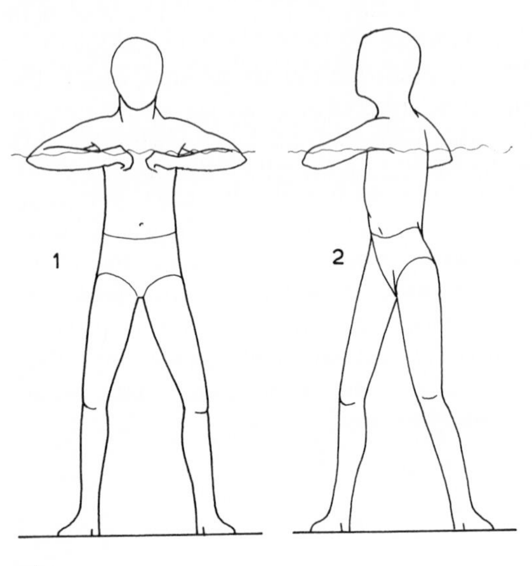

5/4

REASONS FOR DOING IT

To mobilise the whole body, especially the upper back, if done slowly.
To work the muscles in the trunk, if done more quickly and pushing the water.
To strengthen the muscles in the upper back and arms, if done vigorously.
To help balance – however it is done.
To exercise the lungs and the rib case – however it is done.

HOW TO DO IT

Starting position: Place the feet apart, a little bit wider apart than the hips. Let your arms float up to the surface, and your elbows bend.

Move: Slowly turn your head, trunk and arms so as to look behind you, then wind yourself round the other way. Keep the hips more or less facing the front, and get the twist from the spine. Take care to keep your weight over your feet or you will fall over.

Make it harder by using your hands to push aside the water, cupping the palms of your hands and turning them to face the direction of your movement so that you push aside the water as you turn. The more water you 'shift' with your hands, the harder work for your back and chest muscles, and you also make those muscles work harder by keeping your arms more stretched out away from your body. An alternative is to put your hands on your hips, like double tea-pot handles, and twist around using your elbows to push aside the water.

Exercise 5 Side bends (Fig. 5/5)

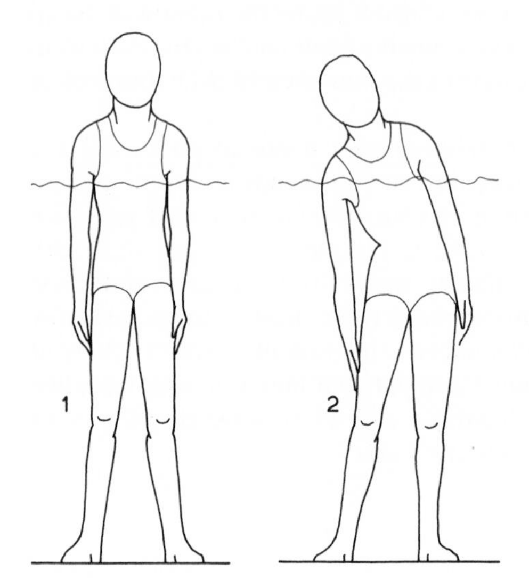

5/5

REASONS FOR DOING IT

To mobilise the joints in the spine and pelvis.
To exercise the trunk muscles.
To reduce pain, if it exists.
For general flexibility, and to 'tone' the waist.

HOW TO DO IT

Starting position: Stand with feet just a little apart, with straight knees so that the fingertips are resting on the outside of the thighs.

Move: Slowly bend sideways from the waist letting the fingers on that side run down the outside of the leg towards the knee. Equally slowly, reverse the movement so as to stand up straight.

Repeat to the same side, trying each time to stretch a little further, but never pushing through pain. After 16 gentle stretches to the same side, then change to the other side. Continue, halving the number you do before changing sides, 16 to each, 8 to each, 4 to each, 2 to each, then alternate sides. Finally, finish the exercise by doing 8 to each side alternately.

CAUTION

If you have pain on only one side of your back, or pain in your leg which your doctor says is referred from your back, then do this exercise bending over to the painful side first. The pain should lessen with each gentle repeat. If it does not get easier, then *stop*.

Exercise 6 Rowing (Fig. 5/6)

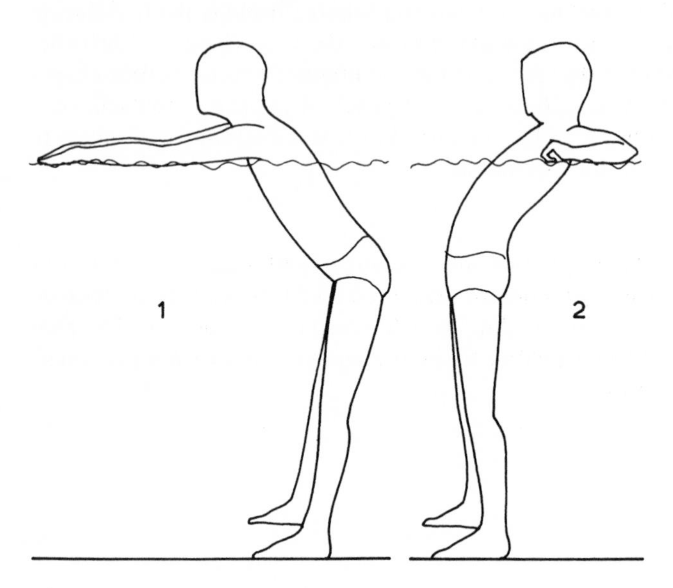

5/6

REASONS FOR DOING IT

For flexibility in the spine, especially the upper back.
For balance.
For mobility in the shoulders.
To work the arm, shoulder and back muscles.

HOW TO DO IT

Starting position: Stand with feet apart and knees straight, in chest-high water.

Move: With both hands, reach directly in front as far as possible without falling forward. Imagine you are pulling on a pair of oars, and pull back as strongly as you can, letting the elbows bend outwards in line with the shoulders but keep the knees straight. Continue in this same direction till the back is arched and you are leaning backwards, but do not topple over. Repeat.

Exercise 7 Bumps and grinds (Fig. 5/7)

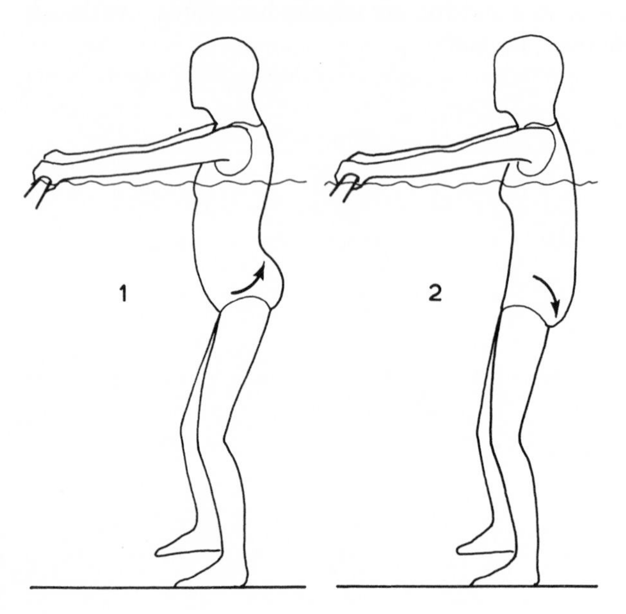

5/7

REASONS FOR DOING IT

To increase flexibility in the lumbar spine.
To prevent and treat lumbar disc problems.
To work the abdominal muscles.
To improve co-ordination in the pelvic area.

HOW TO DO IT

Starting position: Stand facing the side of the pool, holding on just far enough away so that the arms and back are straight. The feet should be as wide apart as the hips, so that the legs are vertical. Bend both knees just a little bit, while keeping the back straight.

Move: The exercise is to flatten and arch the lumbar spine (without moving the knees) so that one is alternately 'humping' and 'hollowing' the small of the back. Only the pelvis should move, the top half of the body being anchored by the arms. (The movement bears more than a passing resemblance to a strip-tease artiste in action.)

Exercise 8 Hula hoop (Fig. 5/8)

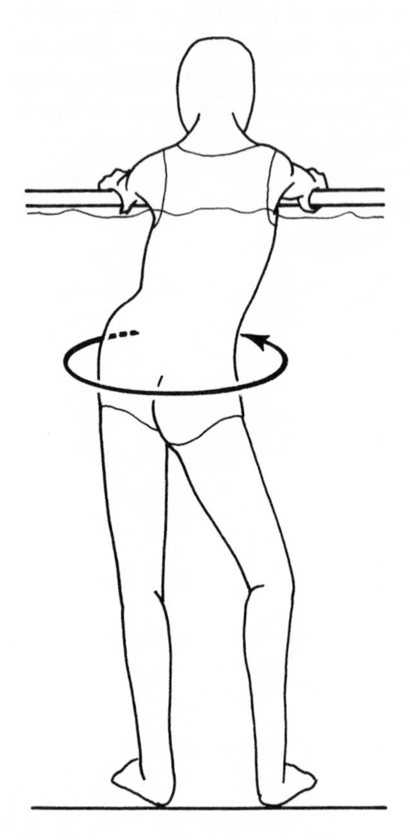

5/8

REASONS FOR DOING IT

To mobilise the joints of the lower spine and the pelvis.
To work the abdominal, pelvic and back muscles.
To improve co-ordination in the area.
Because it is fun!

HOW TO DO IT

This is almost the same as the previous exercise. The starting position is identical, and again, only the pelvis should move, but this time in a rotary direction, as though propelling a hula hoop around the hips (for those of you ancient enough to remember those things). There should be no movement taking place above the waist. Do it several turns in one direction, and then reverse, so that the pelvis has a chance to go both clockwise, and anti-clockwise.

Exercise 9 One-legged ankle rolls (Fig. 5/9)

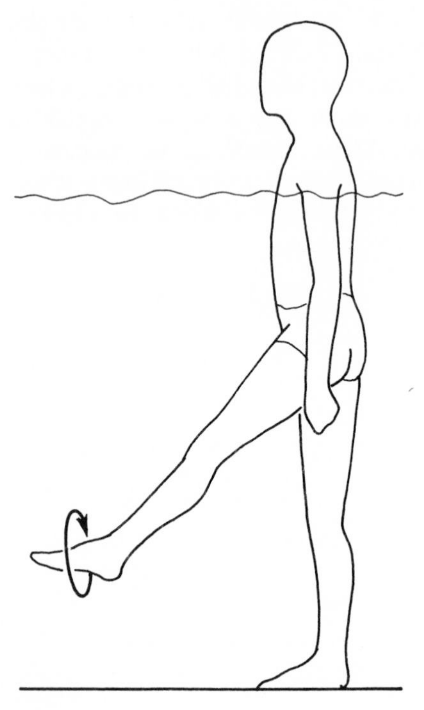

5/9

REASONS FOR DOING IT

To mobilise the joints around the ankle and foot.
To improve co-ordination and balance.
To tone up all the leg muscles.

HOW TO DO IT

Starting position: Stand on one leg (holding on only if necessary). Lift the other leg, keeping the knee straight, so that the leg is at an angle of 45°.

Move: Roll the foot so as to circle the ankle joint. After 16 circles in one direction, reverse the direction of the circle. All the time try to maintain balance. Repeat with the other leg, even if there is nothing wrong with it.

Exercise 10 Curl up and stretches (Fig. 5/10)

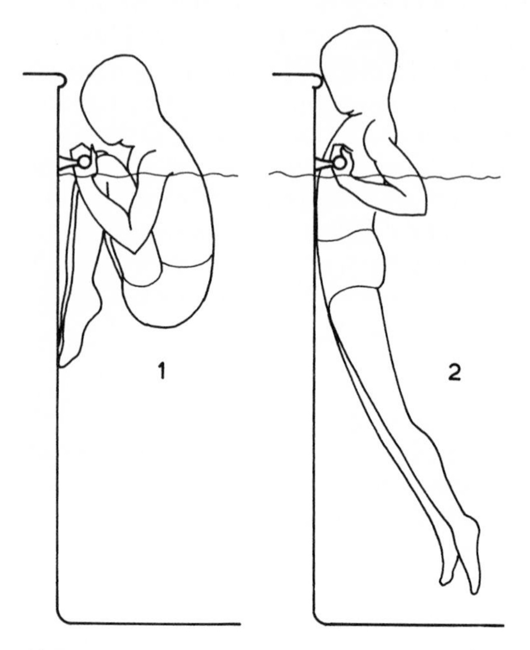

5/10

This exercise can only be done if there is a bar, or an edge to hold on to at the side of the pool or a vacant ladder.

REASONS FOR DOING IT

To strengthen the muscles of the arms, back abdomen and buttock.
To help flexibility of the entire spine.

CAUTION

Do this exercise very slowly and carefully if you have a back problem.

HOW TO DO IT

Starting position: Stand facing the side of the pool and hold on with both hands. It is easier in slightly deeper water.

Move:
1. Bring both knees right up on to the chest, so as to tuck the body into a ball (as in the fetal position). Lower the chin to try and touch the knees.
2. Return to the standing position, still holding on.
3. Stretch both legs behind you (keeping the knees straight and the abdomen touching the pool wall) so as to curve the spine in a backwards direction, arched like a banana. Keep the chin tucked in.
4. Return to the starting position.

FOR KEEP FIT ONLY

Do this exercise in deep water, so that the feet never touch the bottom. It then becomes a graceful swing from the fully flexed to the fully arched position, and is very strong muscle work, especially for the abdominals.

Exercise 11 Ankle rises (Fig. 5/11)

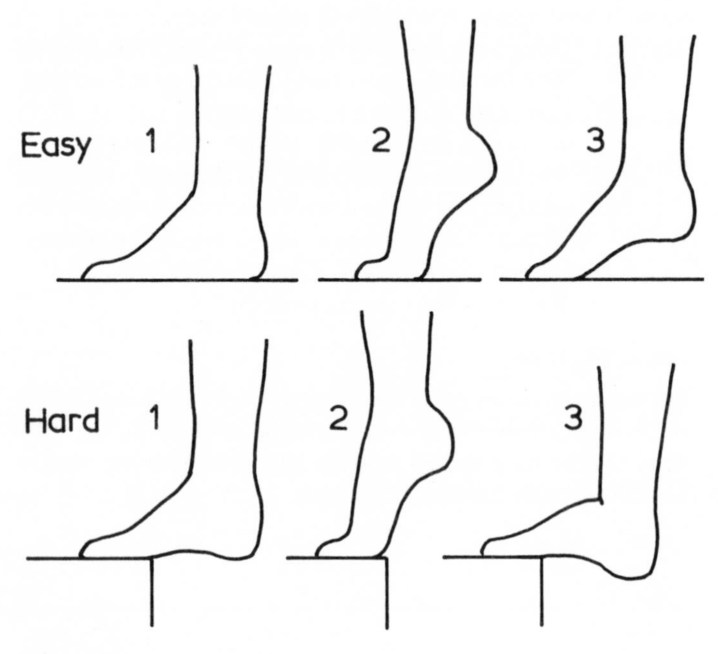

5/11

REASONS FOR DOING IT

To work the calf muscles.
To help with balance.

HOW TO DO IT

Starting position: A. *Easy version*. Stand with feet just a little apart and pointing straight in front of you.
B. *Hard version*. If there is a step, stand with the toes of both feet on the very edge of the step, facing upwards, but with your heels off into space.

Move: Rise on to your tiptoes, then:

A. *Easy version*. Drop on to your heels.

B. *Hard version*. Drop as low as possible, so that your heels are below the level of the step, but your toes are still on the edge of it.

KEEP-FIT VARIATION

Progress to performing the exercise standing on one leg only, holding on only if necessary. This is particularly helpful for balance and co-ordination.

Exercise 12 Knee bends (Fig. 5/12)

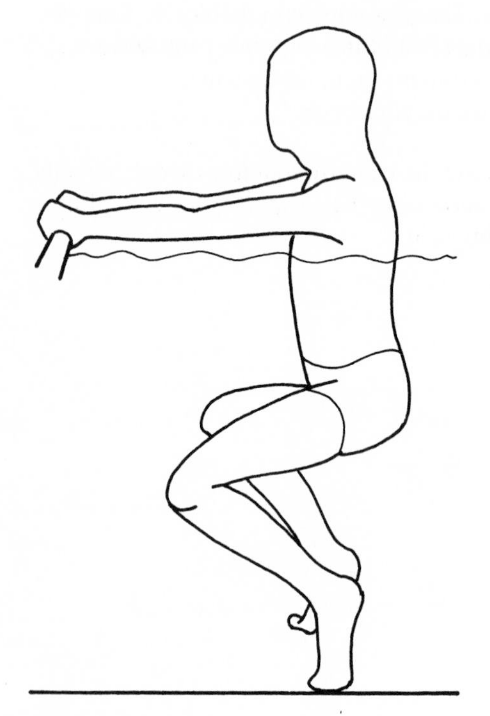

5/12

REASONS FOR DOING IT

To strengthen the thigh muscles.
To work the knee joint.

HOW TO DO IT

Starting position: Face the side of the pool, standing in fairly shallow water. The feet should be a little way apart, and the knees and feet pointing outwards at about 45°.

Move: 1. Stand on tiptoes.
2. Still on the toes, bend both knees outwards, so your shoulders drop down in the water. Keep the back straight, and the weight over the feet.
3. Stand up straight, on tiptoes again.
4. Drop down on your heels.

Exercise 13 Thigh strengthener (Fig. 5/13)

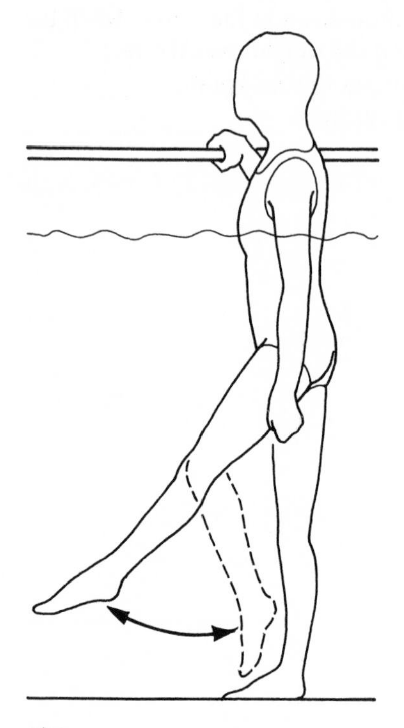

5/13

REASONS FOR DOING IT

To work all the muscles in the thigh, the quadriceps and the hamstrings.

HOW TO DO IT

Starting position: Stand at right angles to the side of the pool, and hold on (if necessary) with one hand. Stand on one leg, and lift up the other leg so that it makes an angle of 45°.

Move: Keeping the knee in exactly the same spot, bend and straighten the lower leg and foot.

VARIATIONS

1. Keep the foot pulled up at the ankle joint, so that the foot is rigid. This is the easy version.
2. Let the foot 'flop', i.e. keep the whole foot absolutely relaxed, so that it drags through the water. This is much harder work.

KEEP-FIT VARIATION

To make this exercise extremely hard, then perform variation 2 wearing a flipper on the working foot.

Exercise 14 Running on the spot (Fig. 5/14)

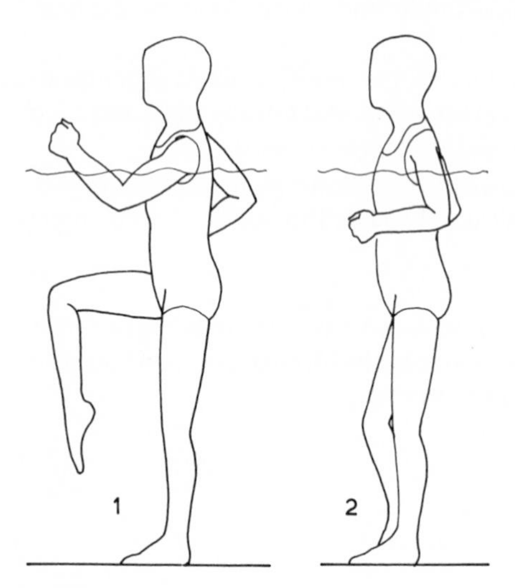

5/14

REASONS FOR DOING IT

For general fitness, and especially for the cardiovascular system.

To work all the muscles in the body, without straining joints with extra load.

This exercise is an exaggerated version of Exercise 1 'Changes' (p. 22). It is exactly what the title says, i.e. running on the spot.

HOW TO DO IT

The salient points are:

1. The movement should be fluid, smooth and rhythmic.
2. With each 'step' the ankle joints should go through a full movement. That is to say, when the leg is off the ground, the foot should point downwards so that the line of the

foot is continuous with the line of the leg, but after landing on the toes, the ankle should then move to allow the heel to drop fully down.

3. The arms and shoulders should move, as when jogging, so that the right arm comes up as the left leg lifts, and vice versa, so causing a rotary movement in the spine.
4. The knees should come up to form a right angle.
5. You should remain 'in balance' all the time.

VARIATIONS

Let the feet come up behind you, so as to try to kick your own backside, but keep the upper body vertical.

Exercise 15 Hip pivots (Fig. 5/15)

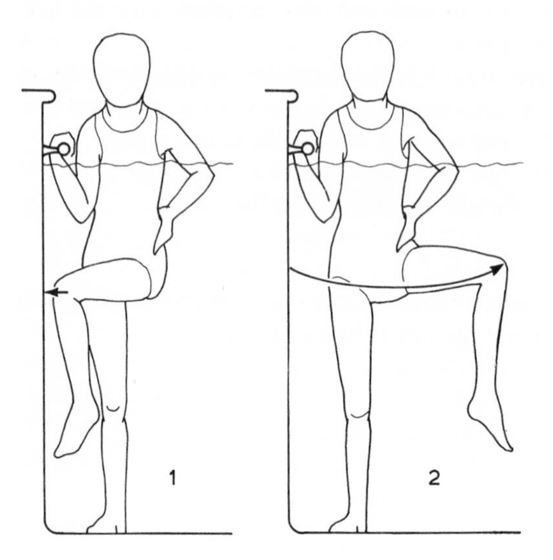

5/15

CAUTION

This exercise is not to be done by people who have an artificial hip joint (arthroplasty).

REASONS FOR DOING IT

To loosen the hip joints.
To strengthen some of the muscles working on that joint.

HOW TO DO IT

Starting position: Stand at right angles to the side of the pool, holding on with a bent right arm, so that the body is near the pool wall. Bend the left leg so that both the hip and knee joints are at right angles. Place the left hand on the left hip bone.

Move: Keeping the lower leg vertical, pivot the left leg round to try to get the left knee to touch the wall of the pool. The left hip bone should not move. When the leg is as far across the body as possible, reverse the direction of movement, so that the knee is brought outwards as far as possible (still keeping the lower leg vertical). To sum up: the point of the knee should draw the arc of a circle going through about 120° (depending on how mobile the hip joint is).

Progression: Start as before, but when reversing the movement stretch the left leg out diagonally behind you, so that it makes an angle of 45° (an arabesque) to the body. Again, the movement should only be in the left leg, but this time there should be fluid change from the turned-in-bent position to the stretched-out-behind position. This exercise should be done slowly and gracefully.

Do not forget to turn round the other way and reverse the limbs to exercise the right hip.

EXERCISES 16 TO 24 (FOR THE SHOULDERS AND ARMS)

Unless stated otherwise, stand in water that is shoulder height or just below.

Exercise 16 Shoulder shrugging (Fig. 5/16)

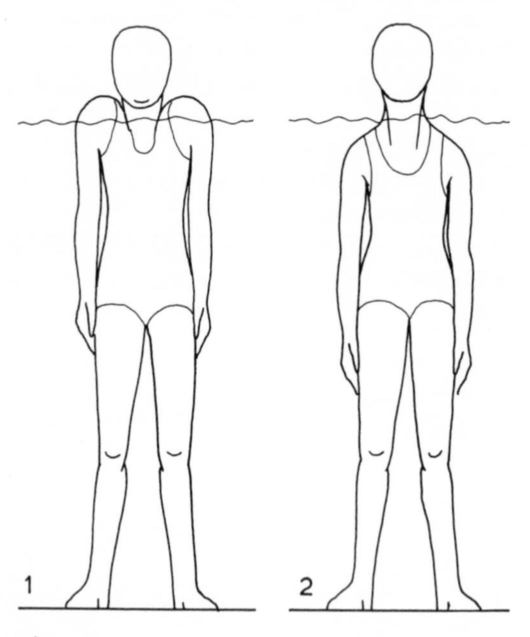

5/16

REASONS FOR DOING IT

To reduce tension in the neck and shoulders.
To mobilise the joints of the shoulder girdle.
To improve posture awareness.

HOW TO DO IT

Starting position: Stand in shoulder-high water, with the feet just a little apart, and the hands by the sides.
Move: Shrug both shoulders thereby lifting them right out of the water and so appearing to shorten the neck. Lower them in time to the music so as to make the neck as long as possible. Take care to keep the chin tucked in. Good posture has lowered, relaxed shoulders.

VARIATIONS

1. Bring the shoulders forwards and backwards (instead of up and down) so as to round them, then stretch them.
2. Combine the up and down with the forward and backward movement so as to circle the shoulders, first in one direction, and then in the reverse direction.
3. Try to move only one shoulder in any of the above ways, while keeping the other shoulder in the relaxed (i.e. downwards) position.

Exercise 17 Elbow cycling (Fig. 5/17)

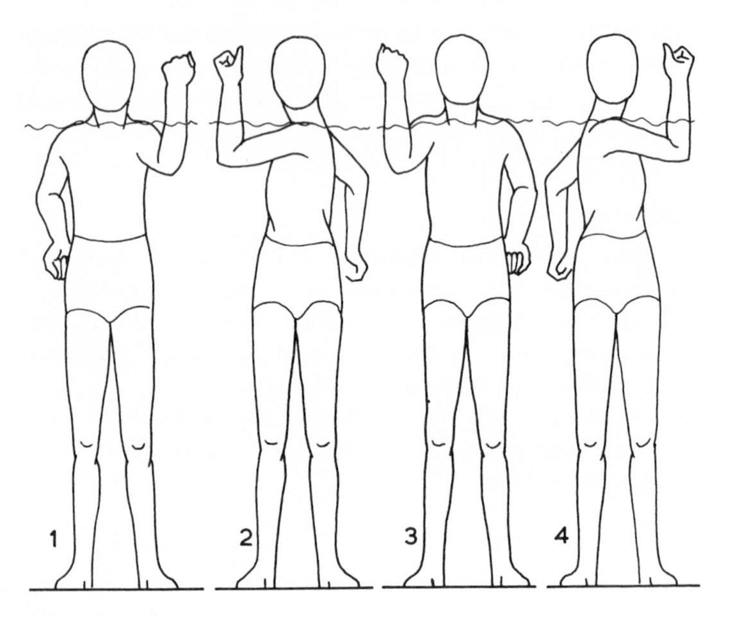

5/17

REASONS FOR DOING IT

To loosen the shoulder and arm joints.
To help co-ordination of arm and shoulder muscles.
To mobilise the neck and upper spine, but proceed very cautiously if there is any pain in the neck.

HOW TO DO IT

Starting position: Adopt the position that a 'body-builder' would take up, if he were displaying his left biceps with his right arm bent behind (1). Now turn your shoulders to the right, without moving your head or feet (2).

Move: Turn your body to the left, while reversing the position of your right and left arms. In other words, go through (3) to end up in (4) which is the opposite of (2). You will find that the elbows have gone through a cycling motion. Continue this cycling alternating between (2) and (4).

Exercise 18 Shoulder girdle bend and stretch (Fig. 5/18)

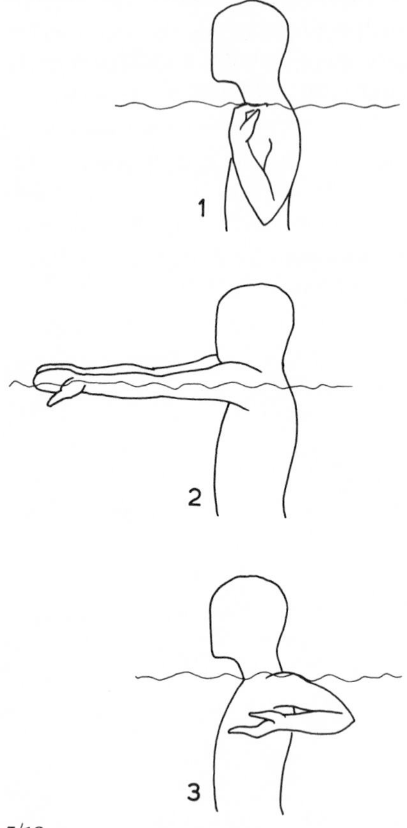

5/18

REASONS FOR DOING IT

To increase flexibility in the arms and shoulders.
To help co-ordination in the muscles of the neck, upper trunk and arms.
To strengthen those same muscles (if done vigorously).

HOW TO DO IT

Starting position: Stand in shoulder-high water with the feet a little way apart and the fingers touching the shoulders.

Move: Stretch both arms in front of you, while turning the palms to face outwards as you reach (so that when your arms are fully extended the backs of the hands are touching each other). As you do this, the neck shortens and the shoulders rise. Reverse the movement, turning the palms upwards and outwards as you go, so that the shoulders are pulled back with the elbows bent behind you. The hands should be close to the shoulders.

Exercise 19 Elbow bends (Fig. 5/19)

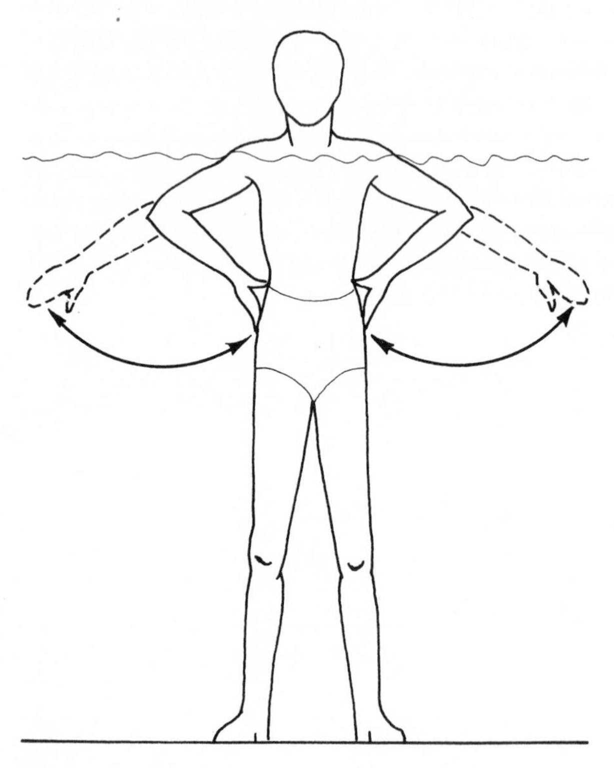

5/19

REASONS FOR DOING IT

For co-ordination, strength and flexibility around the elbow.

HOW TO DO IT

Starting position: Stand with the feet a little way apart and the elbows out, with the tips of the stretched-out fingers resting just behind the hips.

Move: Keeping the elbows in the same place, stretch out the hands and forearms so that arms are straight. The palms of the hands should be facing backwards, and there should be a mild feeling of stretch in the shoulders. The exercise is to bend and stretch both arms.

VARIATIONS

To make it easier, spread apart the fingers.

To make it harder (a) move more quickly or (b) hold an object in each hand, such as a plastic bat or an inflatable armband.

Exercise 20 Passing round or under (Fig. 5/20)

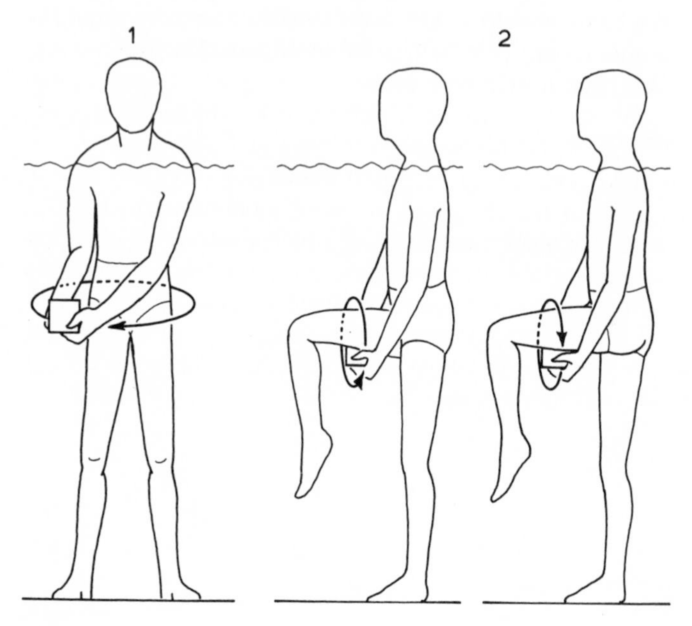

5/20

REASONS FOR DOING IT

To mobilise the shoulder joints.
To strengthen the muscles in the area.
To help with balance and co-ordination.

HOW TO DO IT

Starting position: Stand with the feet wide apart and hold an object such as a flipper (1).

Move: Pass the object from hand to hand so that it moves to make a large circle around the waist. Keep the object moving in the same direction. Reverse directions.

Stand on the left leg (only if your balance is up to it) and pass an object around the right thigh so that it encircles the thigh in a clockwise direction (2). Change legs and pass the object around the left leg in an anti-clockwise direction. The object will have performed a figure-of-eight movement around each thigh in turn. It is rather like juggling with your legs rather than throwing up balls.

VARIATION

The whole exercise can be made much harder work by using an inflated armband as an object. It is then necessary to exert a downwards push to keep the inflatable below the water. But make sure that the downward push comes from the arm, and not by leaning the whole body forwards. The body should remain more or less upright.

Exercise 21 Arm swinging (Fig. 5/21)

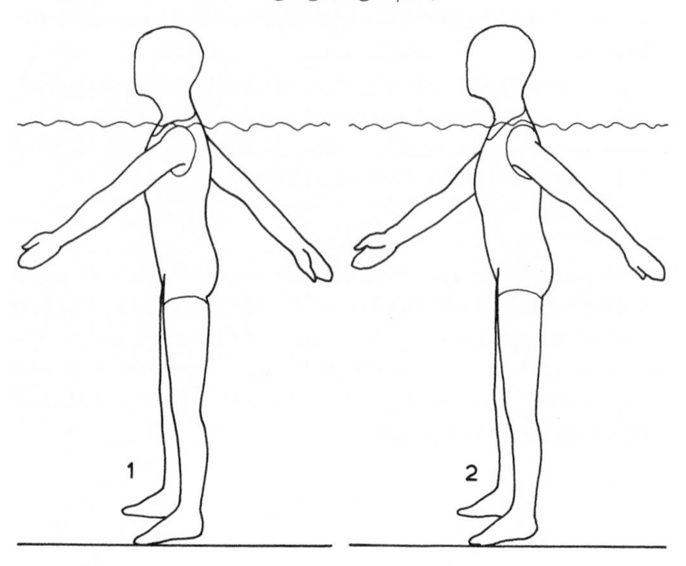

5/21

REASONS FOR DOING IT

To build up strength and mobility in the shoulders and arms.
To work all the postural muscles in the rest of the body so as to hold the stationary position.

HOW TO DO IT

Starting position: Stand with the feet just a little apart, and the hands by the side.
Move: Keeping the elbows straight, and the hands and fingers in a straight line, swing one arm forwards at the same time as you swing the other arm backwards. Reverse directions. This is an imitation of the arm movements when

marching, but the feet keep still. It is much harder work to stand still than to move the legs, especially if the arms move quickly.

Exercise 22 Cutting a diamond (Fig. 5/22)

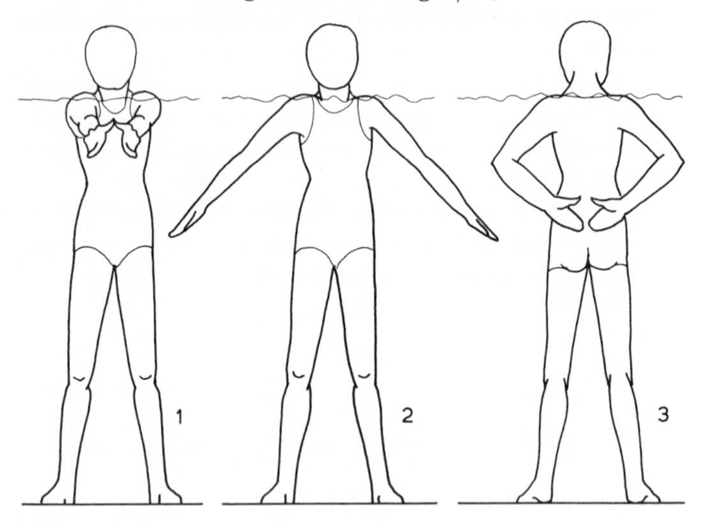

5/22

REASONS FOR DOING IT

To exercise the muscles of both arms.
To mobilise the shoulder joints.
To improve balance.

HOW TO DO IT

Starting position: Stand with the feet apart in shoulder-high water, both hands stretched out in front of you, palms together with thumbs upwards. Now with the thumbs as a 'hinge', separate your palms until they are at an angle to each other of about 30° (1).

Move: For ease of explanation, there are 4 separate stages to this exercise.

1. Keeping the arms and fingers straight and rigid, move them downwards and outwards (making the top half of a

diamond shape) and stopping at 45° to the body (2).

2. Holding the elbows in exactly the same position, bend the lower arm back so the fingers come up just behind the hips (3).
3. Still holding the upper arms in the same position, straighten the elbows so as to return to the same position as in (1).
4. Return the two rigid arms from the angle out at the side to the stretched-out position in front, cutting a reverse diamond pattern through the water as you go.

Exercise 23 Arm walking (Fig. 5/23)

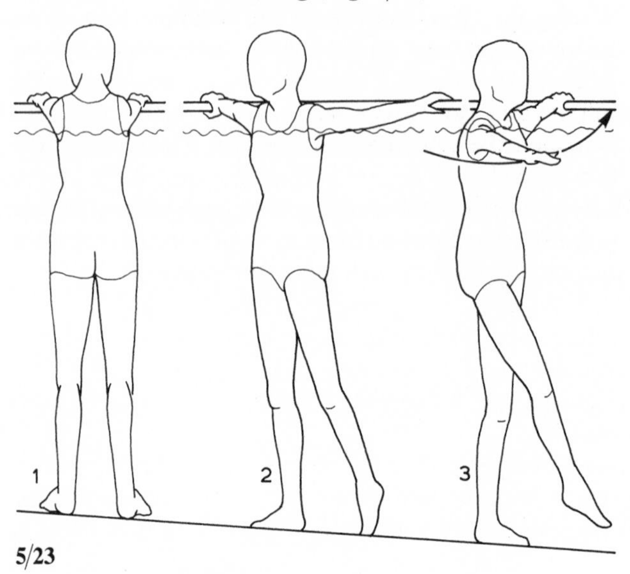

5/23

REASONS FOR DOING IT

To loosen the shoulders.
To improve co-ordination.

HOW TO DO IT

Starting position: Stand facing the side of the pool and hold on with both hands.

Move: The aim of this exercise is to move around the edge of the pool, turning as you do so, but keeping alternate hands stationary as an anchor around which you pivot.

1. When moving to the right around the pool, release the left hand and swing it behind you, followed by the rest of your body.
2. Keep going until the left hand can grab the side, as far away from the right hand as is comfortable, so you are

facing away from the edge.

3. Now release your right hand and continue turning the body in the same anti-clockwise direction until that hand can catch hold of the side. You are now back in the starting position, but farther to the right around the pool side. You obviously have to stop when the water gets too deep for safety. At that time, reverse the direction of movement so that you are moving to the left and performing clockwise circles.

VARIATIONS

The farther apart the hands, the more the stretch on the arms and shoulders.

The quicker the movement is done, the harder you work your muscles.

The maximum stretch to the shoulders is achieved by doing the exercise with the arms as far as possible above the head; to do this either bend your knees or do it in deeper water.

Exercise 24 Breast-stroke arm action (Fig. 5/24)

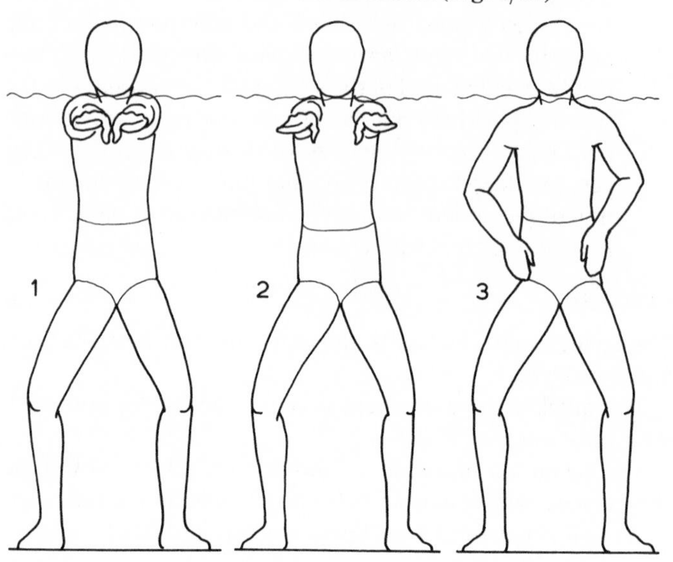

5/24

REASONS FOR DOING IT

To strengthen the arms.

To work the muscles in the rest of the body, to maintain the stationary position in the water.

HOW TO DO IT

Starting position: Stand in shoulder-high water with the feet fairly wide apart and the knees bent. Lift up both arms and stretch them out in front of you, just below the surface. The palms should be flat and the thumbs should be pointing downwards (1).

Move: 1. Both hands move sideways, until the arms are shoulder-width apart (2).

2. Pulling the shoulders downwards and forwards, continue to pull both hands down, but allow the elbows to bend. Keep going until the arms are just in front of the hips (3).
3. Bring the elbows in, and the hands up, straightening the arms as you go so as to return to the starting position.

EXERCISES 25 TO 32 (WALKING EXERCISES)

Exercise 25 Heel strike walking (Fig. 5/25)

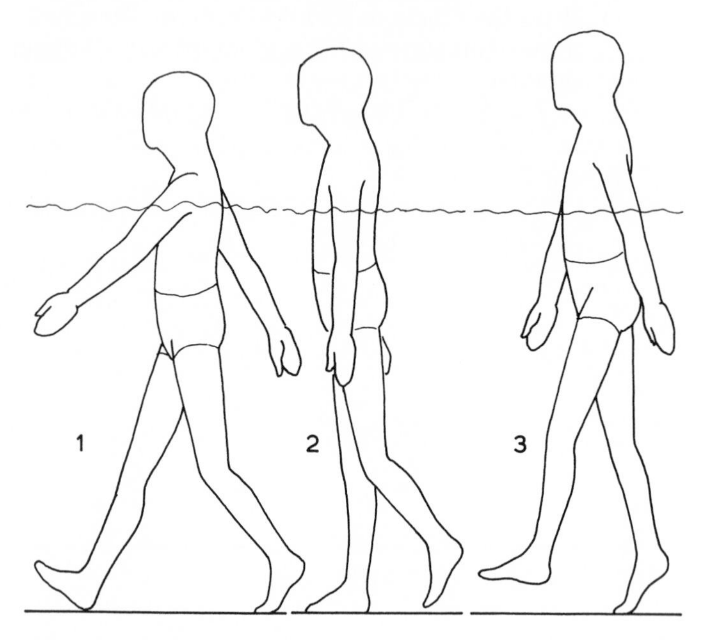

5/25

REASONS FOR DOING IT

To re-educate the normal springy walk that most people lose after a lifetime of wearing shoes. See page 124 for detailed explanation of the function of the feet.

HOW TO DO IT

Starting position: Stand in chest-high water at one side of the pool and prepare to walk across to the other side in the same depth of water.

Move: Walk to the other side of the pool but exaggerate the feet and arm movements as follows:

1. As you bring your foot forward, strike the ground with the heel so that for an instant the heel touches the floor of the pool but the toes are held up.
2. Be aware of the stage when your foot is flat, and all your weight is on it, but the knee is straight.
3. Progress forwards, but get the forward thrust from the toes of your back foot pushing off. This should cause the head to bob upwards.
4. As one leg moves forwards, so should the opposite arm in a pseudo 'marching' motion.

Exercise 26 Slow motion running (Fig. 5/26)

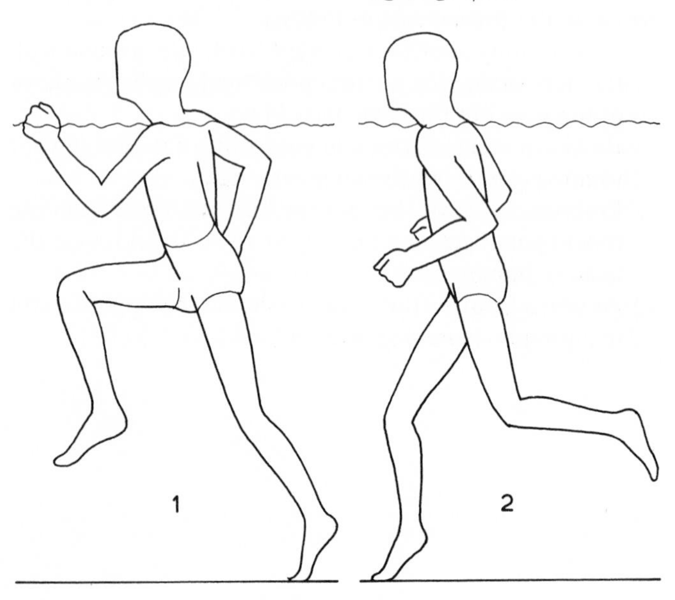

5/26

REASONS FOR DOING IT

To tone up the entire body.
To restore a basic primitive pattern.
To strengthen most muscles in the body.
To mobilise the knees, hips and shoulders.
Because it feels good to do!

HOW TO DO IT

It is quite common to see film in which somebody running flat out has been slowed down. For example, certain shampoo commercials and, of course, the slowed down action-replays of many sporting events. This exercise is to mimic that activity in water. This is perfectly possible in water, but cannot be done at the correct speed on dry land. The salient points are:

1. There is a rotary effect in the spine caused by one foot and the opposite arm coming forwards together. This gives added power to help the forceful forwards propulsion.
2. The stride size is very much greater than when walking.
3. The knees come right up in front, and kick out straight, to give additional power.
4. The toes should exert a strong push-off effect from the floor of the pool.
5. The entire movement should be fluid and graceful.

Exercise 27 Backwards walking (Fig. 5/27)

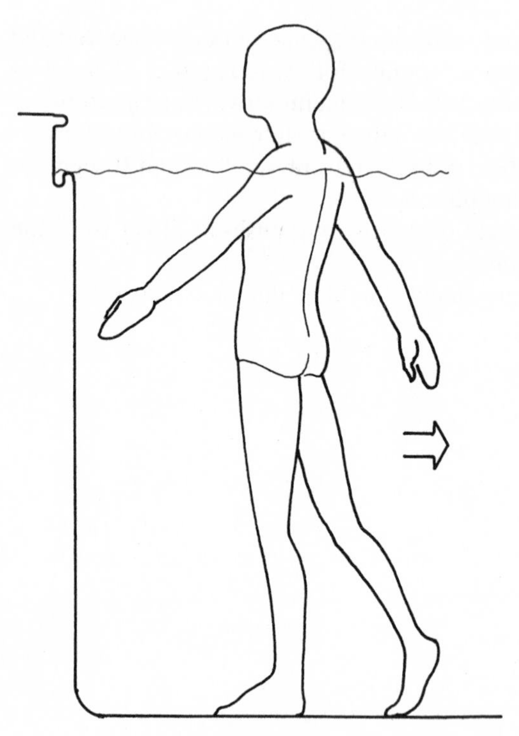

5/27

REASONS FOR DOING IT

To mobilise the back and hips.
To help with balance and co-ordination.
To strengthen the muscles of the thighs and buttock.

HOW TO DO IT

Starting position: Stand facing the side wall of the pool.

Move: Walk backwards to the other side of the pool, observing the following points as you go:

1. Stretch the right leg out behind you as far as you can, but have the right toes make contact with the floor, before the rest of the foot.
2. As the right leg goes back, so also does the right arm, and at the same time the left arm stretches out in front. This gives a twisting feeling in the back.
3. The steps should be as large as possible.
4. The body should remain vertical. Think tall.
5. The movement should be fluid and graceful.

Exercise 28 Sideways walking (Fig. 5/28)

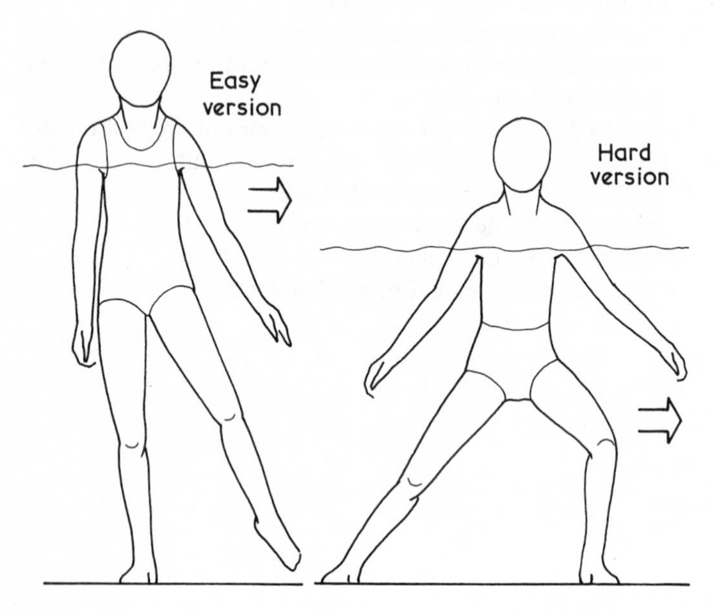

5/28

REASONS FOR DOING IT

To strengthen the postural muscles of the hips.
To mobilise the hip joints.
To strengthen the thighs (hard version).
To help balance.
To help get rid of a limp, if caused by weak hip muscles.

HOW TO DO IT

Starting position: Stand at one side of the pool, facing an end.
Move: A. *Easy version*. To move to the left, lift the left leg and, keeping the knee straight, place it down to the side of you, as far out as you can without having to bend the knee.

Next, bring the right leg in to meet it. Progress as above to the other side of the pool.

B. *Hard version.* Take an enormous stride to the left, allowing the left knee to bend, and transfer your weight on to the flexed knee. Keep the feet and the rest of the body facing forwards. Stand up as you bring your feet together. Progress as above.

Both versions. Come back across the pool to your starting point, without turning round, in order to work both legs equally.

Exercise 29 Braiding (Fig. 5/29)

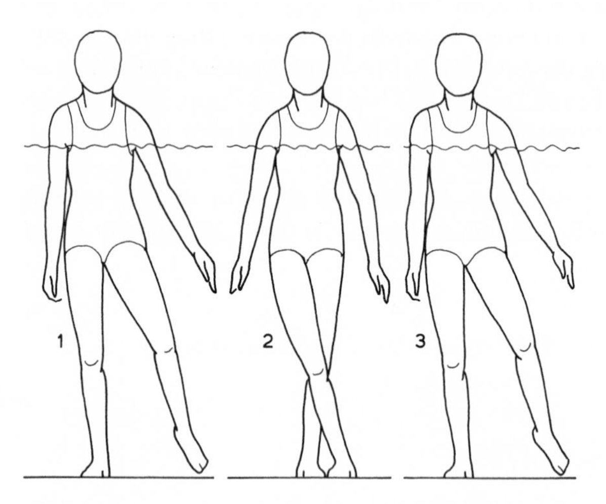

5/29

In the USA, the term 'braiding' means the same as 'plaiting' does in the UK, as, for example, to braid hair. This exercise makes the legs do a loose imitation of the plaiting movement.

REASONS FOR DOING IT

To improve co-ordination and balance.
To strengthen and loosen the ankles.

HOW TO DO IT

Starting position: Stand at one side of the pool, facing one end.

Move: A. *Forward braiding*. Move the free leg out to the side in the direction in which you want to travel. Bring the other foot over *in front* of the ankle so that your feet are touching each other but the right foot is on the left (2). Carry on across the pool, putting the same foot in front at

every step. When you get to the other side of the pool, reverse the direction of movement, putting the other foot in front and taking a wide step to the side with the free leg.
B. *Backward braiding*. This is basically the same movement, but you cross your feet *behind* at the ankles, instead of in front.
C. *Double braiding*. This is a combination of the two movements. On alternate steps, you place the trailing foot in front and then behind the leading one, all the way across the pool.

Exercise 30 Free style walking (no illustration)

REASONS FOR DOING IT

To exercise the brain as well as the body.
Because it is fun!

This is the 'informal exercise'. The aim is to find as many different methods of progressing on your legs from one side of the pool to the other. It is an exercise in ingenuity. For example, one could hop, jump or . . . Count how many different progressions you can think of, but swimming is against the rules! One foot, at least, should touch the floor.

Exercise 31 Running (Fig. 5/30)

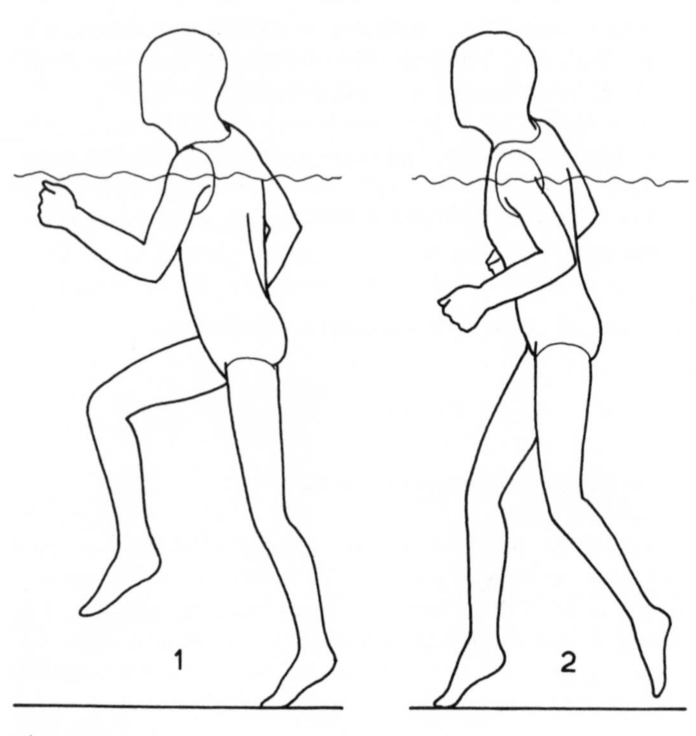

5/30

REASONS FOR DOING IT

To exercise the heart and lungs.
To strengthen all the muscles in the body.

HOW TO DO IT

This exercise is literally what it is called, running across the pool in the same depth of water. The salient points to remember are:

1. The movement should involve the whole body and should look smooth and co-ordinated.
2. There should be a positive arm action that is opposite to the leg action, i.e. as the right leg goes forwards, so should the left arm imitate it in synchrony.
3. This should be a strenuous activity. The aim is to run as quickly as possible, and therefore to get maximum resistance from the water.

The step size should be about the same as for ordinary sprinting on dry land but, inevitably, there will be far fewer steps per minute as the water slows down the movement.

Exercise 32 Resisted walking (Fig. 5/31)

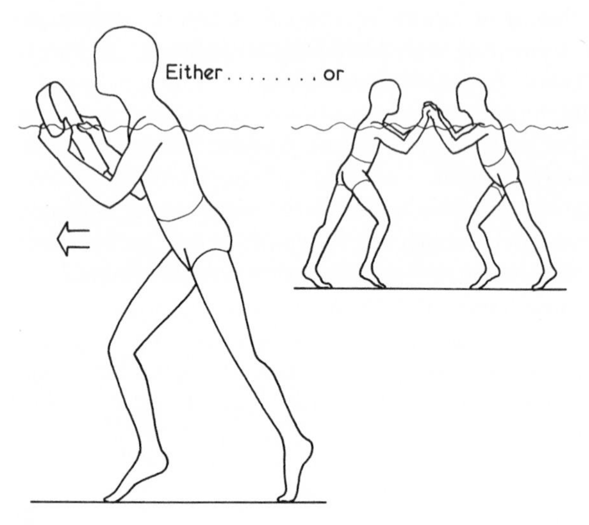

5/31

REASONS FOR DOING IT

To strengthen the arms and back.
To help co-ordination in all the body.
To encourage 'push-off' through the feet.
To strengthen the thighs.

HOW TO DO IT

In order to provide the resistance this exercise can only be done with the help of a float, or alternatively another person. Of the two alternatives, a float is preferable. It is another walking exercise, but not one that is meant to mimic a normal walk. The nearest equivalent in real life would be to push uphill a large old-fashioned pram containing a very heavy baby or a supermarket trolley with a month's provisions.

Move: Hold the float in front of you with both hands so that it is face on to the water, making an angle of 45°, and is partially submerged. Push it forward, keeping your back straight, by getting the power from your knees. The arms have to work hard to control the float. The quicker one walks, the harder the exercise.

If no float is available, then a partner can take over its function. This person must hold both hands of the exerciser, either with intertwined fingers, or with straight hands placed palm to palm. The partner must be prepared to walk backwards, giving resistance to the exerciser, by pushing through their hands. The partner must have a good sense of balance and co-ordination, and adequate strength, so that he or she, can exert sufficient resistance to impede the exerciser's progress through the water, without either of them falling over.

EXERCISES 33 TO 40 (LYING-DOWN EXERCISES)

These exercises are generally performed floating on the back (supine), holding on with both hands so that the hands go from underneath the rail. If possible arrange yourself so that you are floating diagonally in a corner (Fig. 5/32). If there is no rail to hold, then grip the edge of the pool or any other convenient surface. It is also possible to float along a straight edge of the pool, but in order to hold, the arms have to be stretched out from the body, which may be a problem. If there is nothing convenient on to which to hold, then these floating exercises can be done using buoyancy aids such as an inflatable ring or inner tube around the waist.

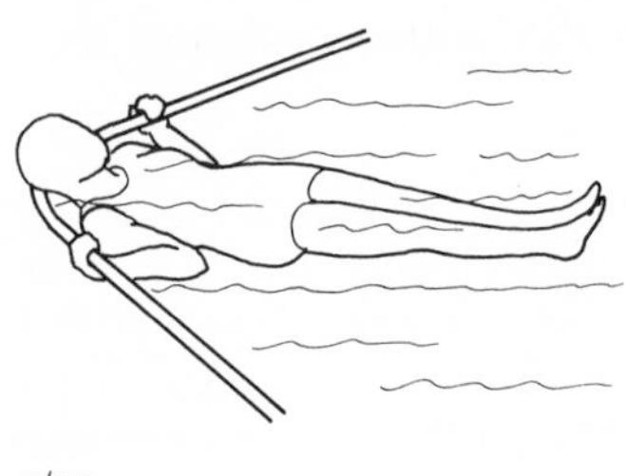

5/32

Exercise 33 Cycling (Fig. 5/33)

REASONS FOR DOING IT

As a warm-up exercise in the lying-down position.
To loosen the knees and hips.
To get the feeling of floating in the water.
To work the abdominal muscles.

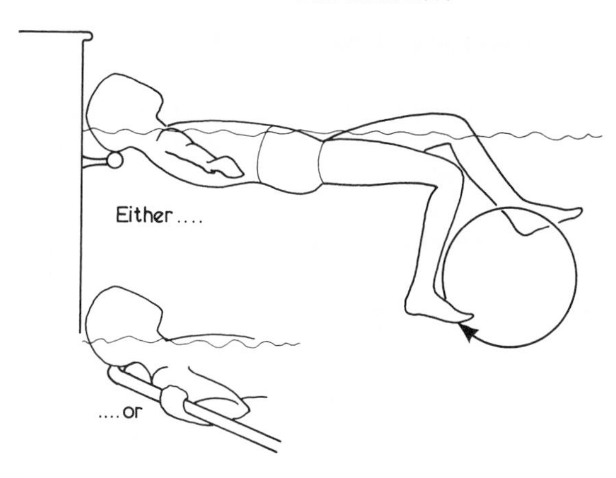

5/33

HOW TO DO IT

Starting position: If possible, do this exercise in the corner of the pool, although it is also feasible to do it along a side surface. Stand with your back to the corner or side of the pool, holding on with both hands, and put your head back so that it is resting on the rail, or in the corner. As you put your head back, so your legs will float up to the surface. Average build, or overweight people will find it very easy to float, but the thin folk will have to work a bit harder to stay there. Most people find that it is more difficult to return to the standing position than to get into the lying position.

Move: By bending at the hips, knees and feet, perform a cycling movement with the legs. The knees may momentarily 'break' the surface, but the bulk of the activity should be carried out under the water. Make the movement rhythmic, and the circles as large as if pedalling a bicycle.

Exercise 34 'Superglue' exercise (Fig. 5/34)

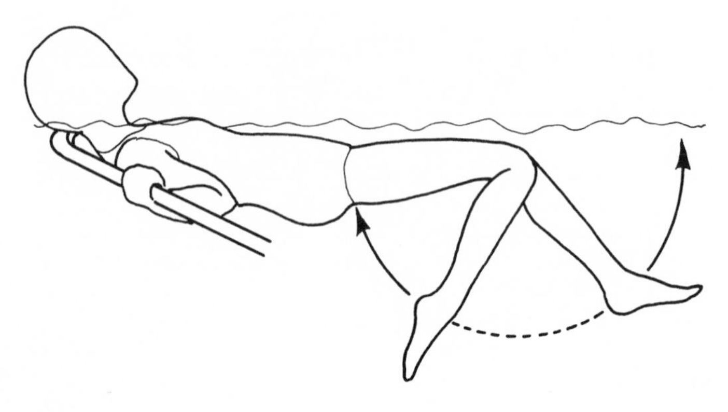

5/34

REASONS FOR DOING IT

To strengthen and stretch the quadriceps muscles (on the front of the thigh).
To strengthen the hamstrings.
To strengthen the abdominal muscles.

HOW TO DO IT

Starting position: Get into the lying position, so that you are floating on the surface, holding on with your hands. The abdomen should be just below the surface of the water, throughout this exercise. Both knees must remain touching each other, as though glued with superglue, and should stay just below the surface of the water.

Move: Bend one knee so that that foot is brought underneath you, as though trying to kick your own bottom. The exercise is to move the two legs at the same time, so that one bends as the other straightens. Remember, the knees themselves should not move, only the leg below the joints.

If you do this exercise correctly, then you will feel the pull in the muscle on the front of the thigh.

VARIATIONS

For added effect, move quickly and forcefully, letting the foot 'flop' in the water, to give an additional 'drag' factor.

Exercise 35 Both legs bend and stretch (Fig. 5/35)

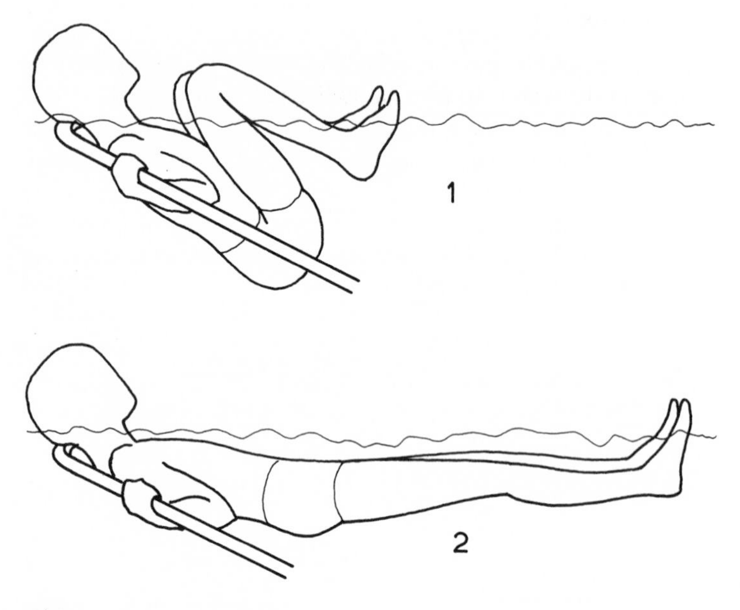

5/35

REASONS FOR DOING IT

For flexibility in the hips, knees and lumbar spine.
To work the abdominal muscles.

HOW TO DO IT

Starting position: Lie on your back (supine) holding on with your hands.

Move: 1. Bring both knees up towards your chin, keeping them firmly together all the time. Try to keep the big toes above the surface all the time. This works the abdominal muscles much more.

2. Still keeping the big toes above the water, push both legs strongly down, leading with the heels, so that you return to the original starting position.
3. Get the feeling of stretch throughout the length of your spine by imagining that a force is pulling on both your feet, as though to pull you away from the edge of the pool. However, you must hold on firmly with your hands so that you do not, in fact, come away from the wall. It should merely be the momentum of the straight push that produces the stretched-out feeling. Even now, your big toes should be 'dry'.

Exercise 36 Twists (Fig. 5/36)

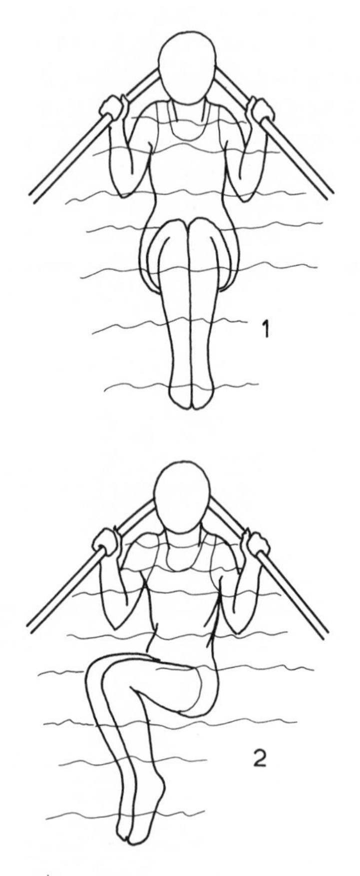

5/36

REASONS FOR DOING IT

To help with rotational flexibility in the lumbar spine. To work the back and abdominal muscles.

HOW TO DO IT

Starting position: Lie in the floating position on your back, with both knees touching each other and bent to a right angle.

Move: Moving both knees together in the same direction, tip them over to one side and then to the other side. The shoulders and arms should remain absolutely still. This causes a twisting in the spine.

CAUTION

If you have back pain, then this will probably help, but do it very slowly and carefully to begin with to make sure that the pain is getting less with each repetition.

Exercise 37 Leg parts and cross overs (Fig. 5/37)

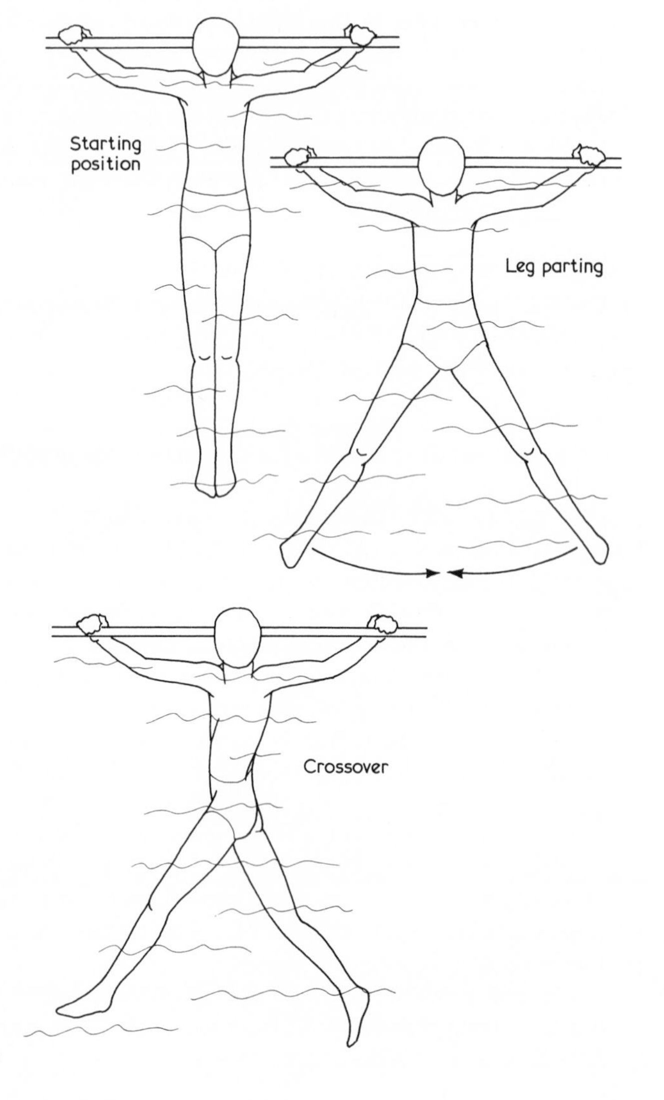

5/37

CAUTION

The 'cross over' part of this exercise must *not* be done by people who have a hip arthroplasty (replacement hip joint). It should be done very cautiously by those who have backache, and should only be attempted if the previous exercise (Twists) can be done without any pain. The beginning of the exercise, the leg-parting section, can be done by anybody.

REASONS FOR DOING IT

To mobilise the lumbar spine and hips.
To strengthen the adductor and abductor muscles of the legs.
To work the trunk muscles.
Because it is very satisfying to do.

HOW TO DO IT

Starting position: Lie on your back as previously described, with your legs out straight in front of you.

Move: 1. *Leg parts*. This is exactly what it says. Part your legs as wide as you can, keeping the feet pointing to the ceiling. Bring your legs together. Try and move as much water as you can with your legs so that you get a 'wooshy' feeling as your legs move through the water.

2. Progress to parting your legs as above, but then, instead of simply bringing them back to meet each other in the middle, cross them over and keep going, so that you are moving them farther away from each other. As your legs part when crossed, allow the upper hip bone to lift up out of the water to let you get a larger movement. When you reach the limit of your 'cross over', then reverse the movement so that the legs are again parted. Next time, 'cross over' the other way, so the other leg is on top and the other hip lifts up.

This can be done as a slow, gentle movement, or as a quicker, stronger movement. It should be rhythmic and not only look good, but feel good.

Exercise 38 Side bends (Fig. 5/38)

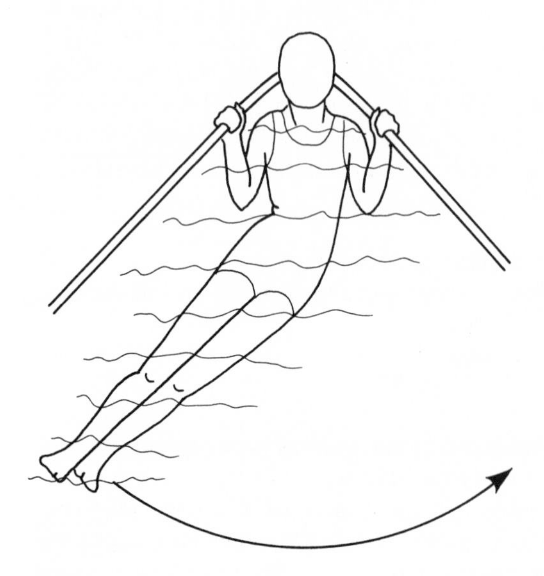

5/38

REASONS FOR DOING IT

To increase the range of sideways bending in the spine.
To strengthen some of the lateral trunk muscles.
To strengthen the arms, as they have to act as stabilisers.

HOW TO DO IT

Starting position: Lie on your back, preferably in a corner, with your legs floating on the surface.

Move: Try to keep your 'belly-button' in exactly the same place, but swing both legs sideways to the same side. Once you are sure that the bulk of the movement is being initiated at the waist, then you may allow your trunk to move a little to the side to allow both feet to touch the wall, if you are doing the exercise in a corner. If you are not in a corner, then only swing round as far as is comfortable. When you have reached your limit (or the wall), then reverse the direction of the waist bend, so that you then move in the other direction. Try not to get a twist in your body when doing this exercise. In other words, keep your legs parallel to the surface of the water, and your feet pointing to the ceiling.

Exercise 39 V-shapes (Fig. 5/39)

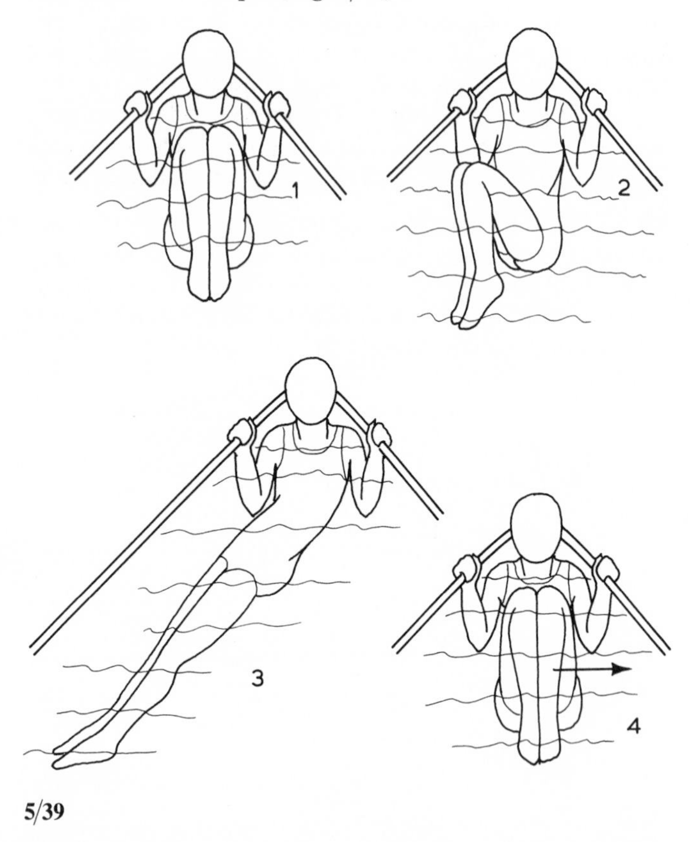

5/39

This is a very hard exercise. It is a combination of the last exercise (Side bends) and exercise 36 (Twists).

REASONS FOR DOING IT

It is a strong abdominal exercise, but it also works most muscles in the body.
For flexibility in the knees, hips and spine.

HOW TO DO IT

Starting position: Lie in the corner, floating on your back. Hold on firmly, and if possible wedge your head into the corner of the pool. Bend both knees up on to your chest.

Move: Flip your bent legs over to the right, stretch your knees out straight so as to touch the right side of the pool with your toes, as far away as possible. From that stretched out position, bring both knees up again on to your chest, flip them over to the left and, in a smooth continuous movement, again stretch your legs out to the left. Finally, bring your knees up on to your chest again and continue, bending, twisting and stretching from side to side. Your body should perform a V-shape in the water.

Exercise 40 The Figurehead (Fig. 5/40)

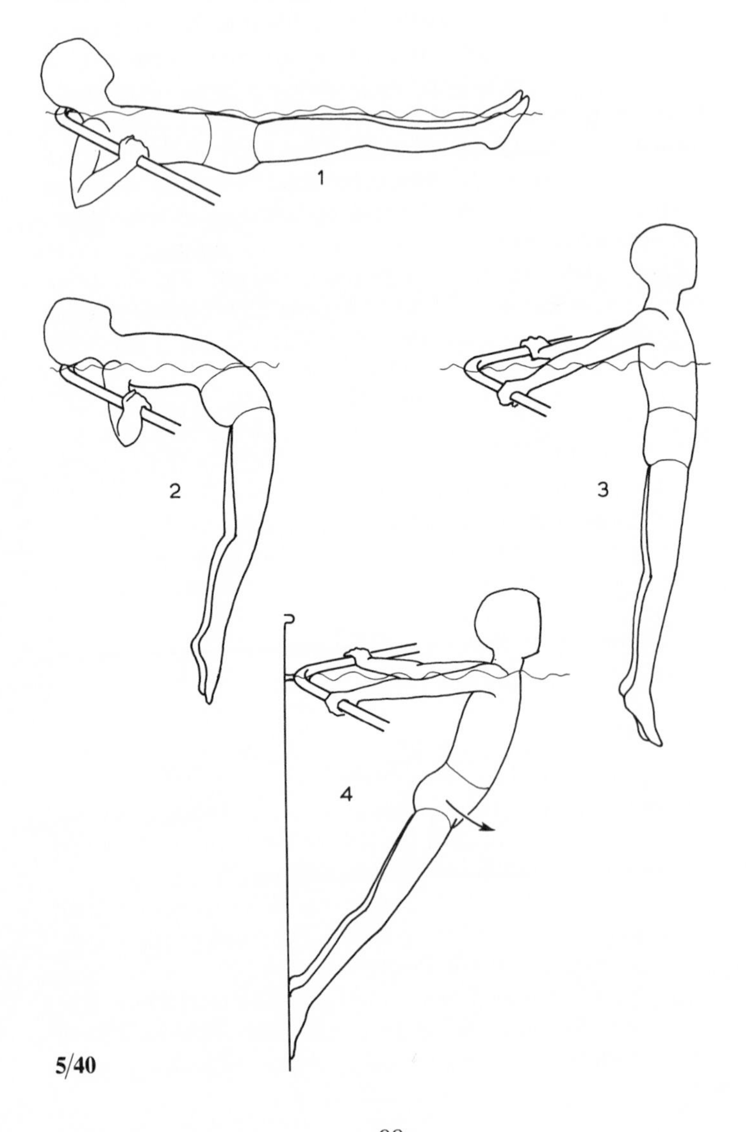

5/40

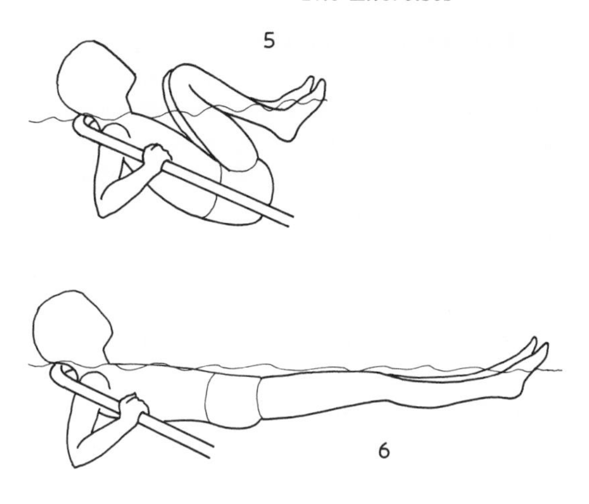

REASONS FOR DOING IT

For flexibility in the whole spine.
To work the back, leg and buttock muscles.
The arm muscles also work to stabilise, and support you.
To help stretch out the spine and give an improved awareness of posture.
For enjoyment, as this is a very satisfying exercise to do.
To relieve backache (*with care*).

HOW TO DO IT

Starting position: This is the usual back lying with your legs floating out straight, on the surface. You must, however, wedge your head against the side of the pool or the rail (if there is one), and hold on under the rail (1).

Move: Keeping your 'belly-button' on the surface for as long as possible, or even lifting it up a little out of the water, arch your back and pull down hard with both legs straight, using your head as a pivot point (2). The work should be done with the buttocks, and the spine and hips should bend back until you are standing on your feet. Now, let go your hands from the rail and push your body forwards, catching hold of the rail from above (3). Keep pushing forwards until you achieve the position in (4). This is an imitation of the figurehead found at the prow of schooners of the *Cutty Sark* era. When holding this position, make sure that the chin is tucked in, thereby exaggerating the line of the spine, and that the back is arched very low down, by thrusting forwards the pelvis. You are then ready to proceed to the last part of this three-part exercise. Pull yourself back into the corner with your hands, change your grip so that you are holding on underneath the rail, wedge your head against the rail, and bring both knees up on to your chest (5). From there the final part of the sequence is to shoot both legs out along the surface of the water, back to where you started. You are now ready to proceed. This sounds a complicated exercise, but it is not, once you have got the hang of it. To sum it up, there are three basic stages:

1. You arch your legs and spine backwards, till you are standing on your feet.
2. You release your grip, catch hold again, holding on from above, and take up the 'figurehead' posture.
3. You pull back into the corner, change grip to the original one, wedge your head, and then bring your knees up then out into the original floating position.

6

Aquarobics for the Fit to stay Fit

FIT FOR WHAT?

The expression 'Keep Fit' is one that is widely used nowadays, but its precise meaning is often confused. It is necessary to ask the question: fit for what? The level and kind of fitness required of a young, professional soccer player is different from that of a mother of three young children who has no home help, or a middle-aged country parson who occasionally cycles around the parish, but doesn't garden and never runs for a bus. When considering fitness this can only be done meaningfully in relation to an individual's requirements, as defined by age, health and life style, and as limited by physical potential. How 'fit' is a good rugby prop forward who can't do up his shoe-laces and requires his wife to cut his toe-nails?

As I see it, there are three basic components of physical fitness, and these are:

1. The efficiency of the cardiovascular and respiratory systems. (The efficiency of other body systems is probably better considered as a matter of health rather than fitness, and if these are below physical potential the remedy is more likely to be in the realm of medicine – in its widest sense – than of exercise.)
2. Muscular strength.
3. Flexibility.

The Western world has become much more fitness orientated in the past few years; indeed, some might feel that in the extreme, fitness has become almost a religious cult. As a physiotherapist, I preach the gospel of 'sensible moderation'. A certain amount of exercise is absolutely necessary to maintain a healthy body, but I do believe that more and more people now are pushing themselves too far, and going beyond that which is reasonable for the mechanics of their bodies. This may produce a sense of well-being, which can continue for some years, but in the long term, if the framework of the body has been mechanically misused, there can be crippling wear and tear in weight-bearing joints.

In the course of my work I deal with sportsmen and sportswomen who have sustained injuries because their training has not achieved a suitable balance between muscular strength and flexibility. Although exercising in water, on its own, is not sufficient training for the élite athlete, it can be very useful as part of a wider training programme. This allows for the development of the muscular and cardiovascular systems, while taking the strain away from joints. As far as average people who just want to keep fit are concerned, then they can probably get all the training they require by using Aquarobics.

CARDIOVASCULAR FITNESS

The heart is a pump containing powerful muscle that can be developed, as can all other muscles, by exercising to make it work a bit harder. This, of course, assumes that there is no underlying disease. However, unlike other muscles, the heart never stops working (beating). The response of the heart to stress is to beat a bit more quickly and/or more forcefully. This stress can be emotional or physical.

In the case of physical stress (exercise), the extra demand on the heart arises because exercising muscles need an increased supply of oxygen and fuel (foodstuffs) and an increased rate of removal of carbon dioxide and other waste products of increased metabolism. The heart satisfies this need by increasing its rate of pumping blood around the circulatory system, through the lungs (to pick up more oxygen and eliminate carbon dioxide), through other tissues (to collect fuel from store, such as fatty tissue, or to deliver wastes for processing, e.g. in the liver) and through the exercising muscles themselves.

This extra activity of the heart itself involves increased muscular activity which, in turn, asks more from the heart in order to increase the circulation through its own muscles (via the coronary circulation). This is to maintain the vital supply of oxygen and fuel for the working heart and to remove waste products, which is why any impairment in the coronary circulation limits the ability to sustain exercise, and why complete blockage by a coronary thrombosis is so catastrophic.

Athletes tend to have a lower resting pulse rate than 'unfit' people, in part because each beat is more forceful and circulates more blood than does the heart beat of someone who is less fit. The rate that the heart beat (pulse) varies in response to demand, and the rate of return to normal on stopping exercise, are the easiest indicators of cardiovascular fitness. Generally, the fitter you are the lower your pulse rate will be at a given level of exercise, and the more rapidly it will return to normal on stopping exercise.

The current concept is that it is good for the heart to be driven to work above its resting rate by body exercise at regular intervals. One much used guide (for the unfit person) is to aim to increase the resting pulse rate to 60 per cent of 220 minus age. For example, for age 40, this would mean taking the pulse rate up to

$$60\% \text{ of } 220 - 40$$
$$60\% \text{ of } 180 = 108 \text{ beats per minute.}$$

There is a sliding scale for this rule of thumb. As just stated,

60 per cent is for the unfit, but the factor for the fit is 70 per cent, and for the athlete 80 per cent. So the 40-year-old athlete would attempt to raise the pulse rate to

80% of 180 = 144 beats per minute

Thus, the unfit exerciser, by exercising three times a week until the heart beats at 108 times per minute, and sustaining that rate for about 10 minutes each time, would keep the entire cardiovascular system 'fit' for the demands that he would be likely to impose on it from time to time by the occasional bursts of exercise in his everyday life. In all cases the pulse should return to its starting rate within 15 minutes.

RESPIRATORY FITNESS

As mentioned above, working muscles (including heart muscle) need oxygen and need to get rid of carbon dioxide. Blood delivers oxygen to muscles and carries away carbon dioxide. This 'spent' blood returns to the heart which then pumps it through the lungs. Here the carbon dioxide is 'blown' off and fresh oxygen is taken up, so that the blood that re-enters the heart from the lungs is 're-freshed', ready to be pumped out again through the circulatory system to the working muscles.

Now, the rate at which you breathe is governed by how 'spent' your blood is, so you will breathe faster if you are doing more exercise and/or if your heart is not pumping blood quickly enough to the lungs, to be 're-freshed'. Another factor is how much gas your lungs can exchange per breath, i.e. lung capacity. The less the capacity, the more you pant on exercise. Capacity can be decreased by disease – bronchitis, emphysema, asthmatic spasm. It can also be increased by exercise of the rib-diaphragm system that expands and contracts the lungs. You do this exercise automatically if you push up your heart rate as described above, because the exercise will also require you to increase your rate of gas exchanges.

If follows from all that has just been said that in order to improve the fitness of the heart and lungs doing Aquarobics, it is necessary to do some of the exercises quickly and vigorously, so as to increase the heart rate and to get a bit breathless. Please, though, remember the earlier warning in this book, and check with your doctor if you have any reason to suspect that you may have heart disease.

MUSCLE STRENGTH

Each individual muscle in the body will only get stronger if it is worked to its 'point of fatigue'. This is common experience. Everybody knows that you have to do repetitive training, often involving the use of weights, to get stronger. In other words, it is necessary to tire out the muscle before it will develop greater strength. Many articles and even books have been written on the scientific complexities of this subject and many exercise physiologists, coaches and trainers devote the majority of their working lives to this problem. However, the key fact is that in order to make muscles stronger, one has to work them repetitively against a load.

Now, if you move slowly through the water, then there is very little load because a submerged limb is effectively weightless. Indeed, for an upward movement the water actually assists the action, so that the muscles work much less than on dry land. But if you move quickly in the water, at a speed that makes you feel the resistance of the water, then you will strengthen that muscle which is doing the bulk of the work.

A muscle can be made tired either by asking it to move a very heavy load a few times, or by moving a lighter load many times. If you are a normal, fit individual, it may be necessary to make the muscles work a bit harder in the water by using flippers, armbands or float boards to give the muscles a larger surface to push through the water. Instructions for this are given with the individual exercises, but generally, the first thing to try when aiming to increase strength is simply to move as quickly as possible through the water, feeling the resistance of the water as you push. This may mean that instead of moving steadily to the music, you need to do a quick forceful 'whoosh' to the water, and then pause, so as to allow the 'beat' to catch up with you.

There are three different ways in which a muscle can work. In technical terms these are static, concentric or eccentric contractions. In a *static* (isometric) contraction, the muscle does not alter in length, but works against a load (as when holding a heavy dumb-bell and displaying one's biceps).

In a *concentric* contraction, the main muscle works by contracting, for example the quadriceps (the large muscle in the front of the thigh) gets shorter in order to straighten the leg to lift the body *up* stairs.

Finally, in an *eccentric* contraction a muscle allows itself to be lengthened in order to control the movement, for example, the quadriceps when going *down* stairs. It is usually gravity that determines whether a muscle is acting in either of the last two categories. However, as previously stated, in the water the gravity effect is eliminated; limbs are weightless. Muscles only work hard in water if they push or pull a limb forcefully through it. Such movement predominantly involves concentric contraction.

Experience shows that muscles are far more likely to develop after-exercise stiffness if they are working eccentrically than if they are working concentrically. As virtually all of Aquarobics is concentric muscle work, it is rare to suffer from stiffness after a session.

FLEXIBILITY

There are two factors determining how flexible a body is. These are the freedom of movement of joints themselves and the stretchability of muscles attached to bones on either sides of joints. As regards the former, in a healthy individual one would not expect joint stiffness. A loss of mobility, because a joint is stiff is either a sign of some (albeit mild) joint disease or a manifestation of extreme old age, where the joint is simply worn out.

It is well known that young children are much more flexible than older people, and that it is normal to lose a certain amount of this flexibility with age. This is mostly due to the tightening of ligaments (which hold bones together across a joint) and the shortening of muscles.

It may be helpful if I clarify what I mean by the word 'stiff'. In this context I am using the word to mean that there is a reduction in the normal range of available movement at a specific joint. As I have just indicated, this can be caused by the joint itself being damaged (and I include ligaments and other structures within the term 'joint') or because there has been a shortening of muscles acting around that joint.

In a keep-fit context it is more likely that any stiffness will be because of tight muscles. It is a good idea to stretch all main muscle groups before and during exercise. This is well known but, unfortunately, often badly done. In order to stretch a muscle to its maximum, the muscle itself should not be in a state of contraction; it should be relaxed. It is important that the stretch should be carried out very slowly (lasting about 5 seconds), and it must not be a jerky movement.

Muscle stretching exercises are not specifically included in the exercise section of this book, although joints are often taken through a full range of movement, which may well involve stretching individual muscles. Aquarobics are dynamic rhythmic exercises and by their very nature do not stretch muscles to their fullest extent as it is impossible to carry out an active rhythmic exercise while at the same time doing a slow relaxed stretch. None the less, 'mobility' is often given as one of the aims of the exercises and, if so, then tendons and to some extent muscles, are being stretched. This is especially true of the trunk.

Since the main exercises in the book are not specifically for muscle stretching, the athlete or keep-fit participant might like to add the following stretches to selected exercises, either in or out of the water. All these stretches should be done very slowly and smoothly, about 3 to 5 times each.

Hamstring stretch (Fig. 6/1)

When stretching the right leg, put that leg with its knee straight on a step, or a rung of a ladder, so that it is about 30cm (12in) off the ground. Slowly reach forward so as to

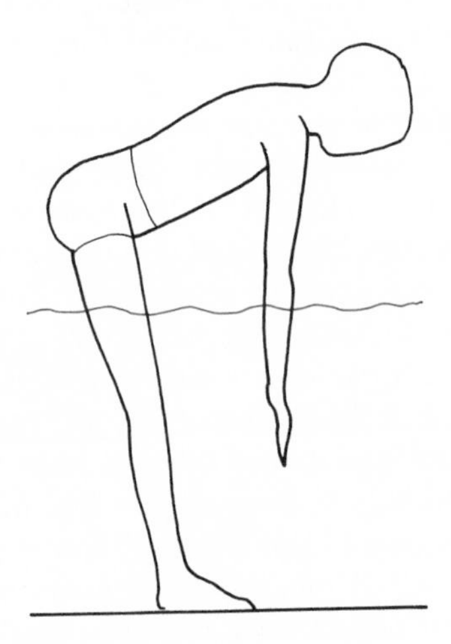

Fig. 6/1 Hamstring stretch

touch the right foot with both hands, while keeping both knees straight. If done correctly, you will feel a pull in the muscles at the back of the thigh. Repeat with the left leg.

If no step or rung is available, then an alternative is to stand in shallow water, and bend slowly forwards to try to touch the toes, keeping both knees absolutely straight (Fig. 6/1). This is much more effective if done keeping the back also absolutely straight. To do this you lean forward, but get the feeling of keeping your bottom stuck out.

Quadriceps stretch (Fig. 6/2)

Stand on one leg, holding the other foot around the ankle with the hand on that side, so that the leg is held behind you.

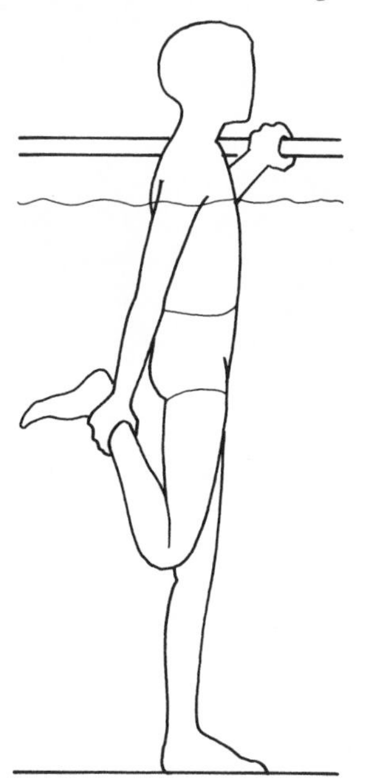

Fig. 6/2 Quadriceps stretch

While keeping the body upright, slowly pull that leg farther back. You will feel a pull on the muscles at the front of the thigh. Repeat with the other leg.

Psoas stretch (Fig. 6/3)

This can only be done in the water if there is a step or a suitable rung of a ladder on which to put your foot. Otherwise do it on dry land.

Put the right foot on a step about 35cm high, with the knee bent, and put the other leg as far behind you as possible. Bend your body forwards, but keeping the upper body vertical. Slowly stretch, and you will feel the pull in the groin. Repeat with the left foot on the step.

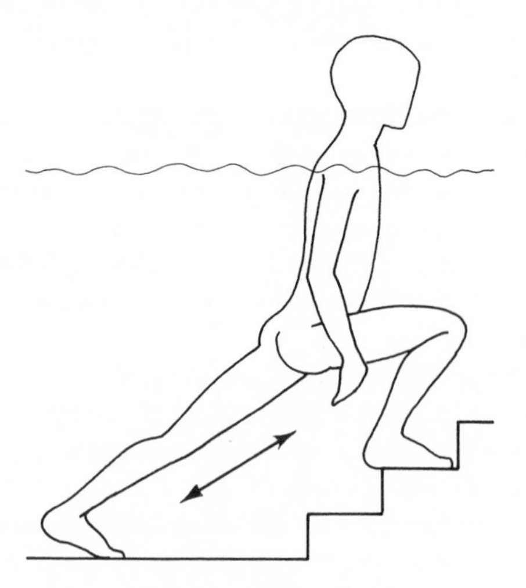

Fig. 6/3 Psoas stretch

SUGGESTED EXERCISES FOR A KEEP-FIT PROGRAMME

All the exercises in this book can help to keep you fit, especially if they are done quickly and forcefully. However it would probably take too long to do them all in a single session, even a very long one. In any case, the first few sessions should be relatively short and undemanding, to conform to the principle of sensible progression. Some are more suitable than others for the fully fit person and the exercises that are listed below form the basis of a suitable selection.

From experience 30 minutes has proved to be an optimum time for a session performing these exercises. This allows for 10 exercises to be performed for 3 minutes each. The selected exercises ensure that all the muscles of the body are being used and that all joints are put through their full range of movement.

Moreover, these exercises need no special pool equipment such as rails. The one exception to this is the cycling exercise. For this it is necessary to hold on to something to stabilise the upper half of the body. Alternatively, if no fixed point is available, it can be performed by wearing an inflatable ring. It can also be done by having your trunk supported by another person.

All of this means that, for the fit person, Aquarobics can even be done in the sea, providing the sea floor is sandy or you are wearing water shoes, but watch out for big waves, or other hazards such as rocks. You will need to have a really good sense of balance in the sea, because the surface is uneven and waves and currents create added difficulties. You must also be careful not to get cold.

The exercises

1. Exercise 1 Changes (p. 22). Progressing very quickly to
   Exercise 14 Running on the spot (p. 48).
2. Exercise 2 Leg swinging (p. 24).
3. Exercise 3 Sideways leg swinging (p. 26).
4. Exercise 4 Corkscrew (p. 28).
5. Exercise 5 Side bends (p. 30).
6. Exercise 20 Passing round and under (p. 60).
7. Exercise 26 Slow motion running (p. 72).
8. Exercise 31 Running (p. 80).
9. Exercise 33 Cycling (p. 84) (see note above).
10. Exercise 37 Leg parts and cross overs (p. 92).

7

Aquarobics for the Unfit to get Fit

BACK PAIN

Almost everybody has a pain in their back at some time in their life. There are many reasons for this, but most back problems are of a mechanical nature. There are numerous treatments available from a variety of practitioners – both of the orthodox and the alternative kind. Back pain has been treated by exercise for a considerable time. I treat patients with backache by manipulation, electrical treatments and exercises. I do believe that if a full range of movement can be restored, and if the muscles recover their normal power after a 'back' incident, and finally, if the spine is used in the way that nature intended, then the likelihood of a recurrence is significantly reduced.

I have found water an essential medium for the rehabilitation and treatment of back disorders, whatever their underlying cause. Having said that, I must add that if the cause of the back pain is a tumour, then obviously more treatment than just Aquarobics is needed. It is essential to check the cause of the back pain with your doctor. Certain back lesions require expert supervision, and care must be taken before 'rushing' at the exercises in this book.

It is helpful to know a little bit about the anatomy of the region so that one can understand in mechanical terms, what is happening (Fig. 7/1).

The spine is an engineering miracle. It is made up of 33 vertebrae with shock-absorbing discs (the intervertebral

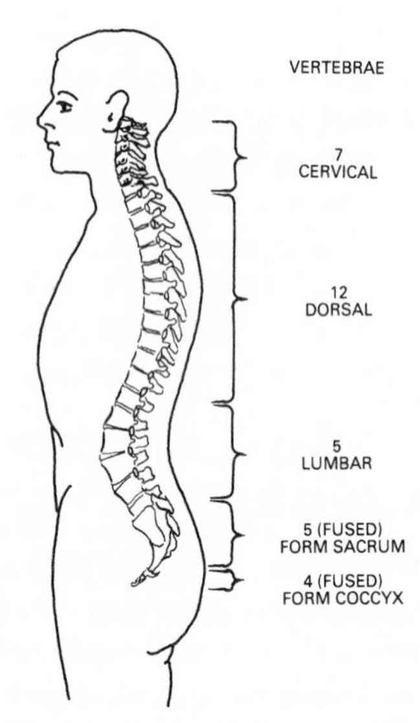

Fig. 7/1 Simplified anatomy of the spine

discs) between the upper 24. The spine is arranged in three curves: cervical (neck); dorsal (chest); and lumbar (lower back). These curves help to absorb the stress put on the human spine because of man's erect posture. In addition, the spine is the basic framework of the body upon which everything else is anchored. It is also a flexible tunnel protecting the spinal cord and enabling nerves to be distributed to the rest of the body.

In a machine, if one small part functions wrongly, then the working of the whole can be deranged. In the same way, if any structure around the spine is damaged, then the function of the whole is impaired. Damage and pain usually seem to result from sudden stress, but this stress may be the last straw to an already insidiously damaged spine. Our bodies evolved over aeons of time to cope with the demands of man but only recently have we abused nature's design by an accumulation of minor wear and tear, such as poor working position, bad posture, being overweight and twentieth-century living.

Aquarobics is especially helpful for the treatment of this type of underlying chronic back lesion (which is by far the most common situation), whether or not it presents as an acute episode. When in water, there is no weight passing through the spine, the discs are not compressed and it is possible to mobilise, strengthen and restore some degree of normal function.

Suggested exercises for back pain

If you are in pain, then proceed extremely slowly and carefully. Do not attempt to exercise for more than 15 minutes the first time. Remember, if the exercises are helping you, then the pain should subside. Please refer back to the first principle on page 9. If in doubt about the reason for your pain, then seek professional help.

BASIC EXERCISES

1. Exercise 1 Changes (p. 22).
2. Exercise 2 Leg swinging (p. 24). Use great care. It may hurt either lifting forwards or backwards, but it is unlikely to be both. Should get easier on gentle repetitions.
3. Exercise 4 Corkscrew (p. 28). Very helpful. Usually reduces the pain.
4. Exercise 5 Side bends (p. 30). Do it bending over to the most painful side first, about 8–10 times, then do the same number to the opposite side.
5. Exercise 7 Bumps and grinds (p. 34). This one is useful to do in and out of the water. When 'dry' do it lying down on your back, with your knees bent and the feet on the bed (or floor). Any pain should get less on repetition.

This is strong medicine for disc problems, so take it carefully. Continue as indicated on page 35.

6. Exercise 8 Hula hoop (p. 36). Do not attempt this exercise if the previous exercise hurts.
7. Exercise 26 Slow motion running (p. 72). Should be no problem.
8. Exercise 27 Backwards walking (p. 74).
9. Exercise 33 Cycling (p. 84).
10. Exercise 36 Twists (p. 90).

ADDITIONAL EXERCISES FOR BACK PAIN

1. Exercise 3 Sideways leg swinging (p. 26).
2. Exercise 6 Rowing (p. 32).
3. Exercise 10 Curl up and stretches (p. 40).
4. Exercise 12 Knee bends (p. 44). Even though this works your knees and not your back, it is helpful because it is necessary to have strong thigh muscles to protect your back when you lift.
5. Exercise 14 Running on the spot (p. 48). For general fitness, but also for the back, if you lift your knees up high as you run.
6. Exercise 15 Hip pivots (p. 50).
7. Exercise 16 Shoulder shrugging (p. 52).
8. Exercise 30 Free style walking (p. 79).
9. Exercise 31 Running (p. 80).
10. Exercise 34 Alternate knee bends ('Superglue' exercise) (p. 86).
11. Exercise 35 Both legs bend and stretch (p. 88).
12. Exercise 37 Leg parts and cross overs (p. 92).
13. Exercise 38 Side bends (p. 94).
14. Exercise 39 V-shapes (p. 96).
15. Exercise 40 The figurehead (p. 98).

HIP PAIN

If you suffer from pain in the region of the hips, this may well not be caused by a lesion in those particular joints. It is quite common to have buttock or groin pain which is referred from the spine, or from the joints between the spine and the pelvis. Occasionally, pain that seems to be coming from the hips can be a symptom of a more serious cause. It is therefore essential to check with your medical practitioner before embarking on Aquarobics. If you are told that the reason for your pain is a mechanical problem in that joint itself, then it is worth while giving Aquarobics a try.

Osteoarthritis of the hip joints in its early stages can be helped by exercising in water, but in the more advanced stage it can only relieve the pain temporarily. (Indeed, there is a danger of doing too much in the water without having the warning effect of the pain to remind you to stop. This can stir up the pain so that it comes back with a vengeance later on.) However, it does help to keep the muscles in trim until such time as the hip can be operated on. It also 'reminds' the brain of what it is like to walk without a limp, as the non-weight-bearing effect of the water enables a more normal gait. Do remember, though, to begin slowly and gently and not for too long.

Aquarobics are very useful when recovering after a hip arthroplasty. However, there are one or two words of caution. Firstly, check with your surgeon if the operation is less than a month before. Secondly, you will have been told by the physiotherapists who saw you when you were in hospital that you must not cross your legs, and you may also have been given guidelines about movement. Needless to say, you must observe these when in the water, as much as when on dry land. Exercise 15 Hip pivots should *not* be done by anybody who has had a hip arthroplasty, as that exercise brings the leg into the very position which should be avoided.

SUGGESTED EXERCISES FOR OSTEOARTHRITIS OF THE HIP

1. Exercise 1 Changes (p. 22).
2. Exercise 2 Leg swinging (p. 24).
3. Exercise 3 Sideways leg swinging (p. 26).
4. Exercise 5 Side bends (p. 30).
5. Exercise 12 Knee bends (p. 44).
6. Exercise 13 Thigh strengthener (p. 46).
7. Exercise 25 Heel strike walking (p. 70).
8. Exercise 26 Slow motion running (p. 72).
9. Exercise 33 Cycling (p. 84).
10. Exercise 34 Alternate knee bends ('Superglue' exercise) (p. 86).
11. Exercise 35 Both legs bend and stretch (p. 88).
12. Exercise 36 Twists (p. 90).
13. Exercise 27 Backwards walking (p. 74).
14. Exercise 28 Sideways walking (p. 76).
15. Exercise 31 Running (p. 80).
16. Exercise 32 Resisted walking (p. 82).

The following three exercises must NOT be done if you have an arthroplasty, but are otherwise very useful.

17. Exercise 15 Hip pivots (p. 50). Note caution above.
18. Exercise 29 Braiding (p. 78). Note caution above.
19. Exercise 37 Leg parts and cross overs (p. 92). Note caution above.

KNEE PAIN

Pain around the knee is a very common problem. There can be a multitude of reasons for this. It is important to know the diagnosis of knee pain, as there are a few conditions which should not be treated by exercise, but instead require to be rested, and others which need the attentions of an orthopaedic specialist. Knees which are extremely painful, swollen or angrily inflamed, should be rested and not subjected to Aquarobics, unless the latter is part of a therapeutic session conducted under the supervision of a physiotherapist.

Quadriceps and the knee

The major muscle acting on the knee joint is the quadriceps, which is found at the front of the thigh. This muscle straightens a bent knee against a resistance, and is therefore very active maintaining the upright posture against gravity. If this muscle is at all weak then it prevents the knee joint from functioning normally. One sign of quadriceps weakness is pain or difficulty going up or downstairs. This is likely to get progressively worse, since there is a reflex which operates, which causes the quadriceps muscle to get weaker if there is anything wrong with the knee joint. This effectively causes a vicious circle to set in (Fig. 7/2).

The only way to break into this vicious circle is to strengthen the quadriceps in such a way as not to cause pain or increase any swelling that may exist. This will mean doing a

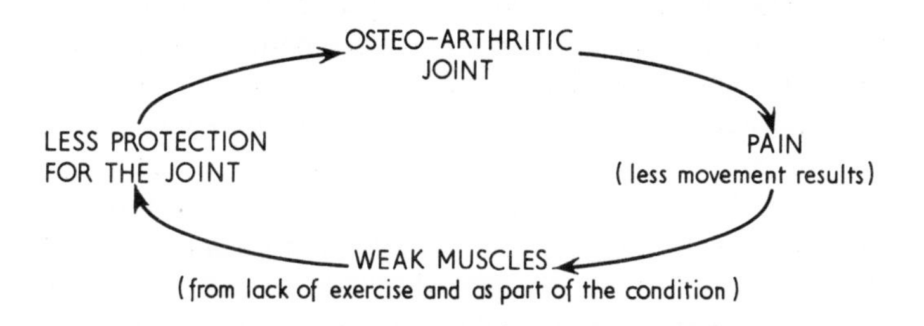

Fig. 7/2 The vicious circle of arthritis

certain amount of exercise on dry land, such as 'straight leg raising'. To do this you lie propped up, and tighten your thigh muscles. Then, keeping the whole leg absolutely straight, you lift it up slowly until it is about 25cm (10in) above the surface, then hold it while you count five, and then slowly lower it back on to the surface. If this is easy, attach an appropriate weight (about 1kg (2lb) to start) over the ankle and continue. You should gradually build up, aiming to achieve 50–100 lifts with the leg (with appropriate weights if necessary). Allow yourself brief pauses between every 10 lifts.

Aquarobics is another way to strengthen the quadriceps. Exercise 12 Knee bends (p. 44) and Exercise 13 Thigh strengthener (p. 46) are specifically designed for that purpose. Most of the other exercises involve the quadriceps to a lesser extent. As already stated, Aquarobics exercises are non-weight-bearing and are therefore much less likely to aggravate an irritable knee joint than similar dry-land exercises. In chest-high water one is almost weightless and therefore there is no compression force jarring the bone ends together.

The swollen knee

In the introduction (pp. 3–5) the therapeutic advantage is discussed of allowing a body to move in a normal way through water when it is unable to do so on dry land. There is no doubt that knee problems are particularly amenable to aquarobic-type exercises. One incidental finding is that Aquarobics helps to reduce swelling and hence make the joint much more comfortable. It may not be anything magical in the actual exercises that produces this effect, it is probably simply that the pressure of the water on a swollen limb, combined with the 'pump' effect of muscles, disperses excess body fluid (which accounts for the swelling) by squeezing and pumping it away back to the main body compartments so that it can be disposed of in the usual way. All of the walking exercises (Exercises 25–32 pp. 70–82) will be useful to reduce swelling, and they should be done in addition to the two exercises listed above.

Suggested exercises for knee problems

If the knee is swollen and painful, but your doctor or physiotherapist tells you that it has reached a stage when you can start exercising in water, then you must do very little the first time. Probably walking in water that is between chest and shoulder height is the most helpful single activity. After you have done this for a little while you will probably be able to move into slightly shallower water and continue there. You may now be able to do the first few of the specific knee exercises listed below. But do remember to take it gently, and not to push through pain!

BASIC EXERCISES

1. Exercise 1 Changes (p. 22). You will only be able to do this if there is a certain amount of bend in the bad knee. If this hurts, then go straight on to the next exercise.
2. Exercise 2 Leg swinging (p. 24). Start off by swinging the bad leg, remembering that you must tighten up the thigh muscles so as to keep the knee really straight. (Do not forget to keep your foot pulled up at the ankle, or else you will stub your toes.) Always repeat with the other leg, as your bad leg will still be working to hold you in the upright posture.
3. Exercise 9 One-legged ankle rolls (p. 38). This mobilises the foot, while working the knee muscles on the supporting leg.

4. Exercise 12 Knee bends (p. 44). Start off gently in water that is fairly shallow. Progress into shallower water. (This exercise has already been mentioned in connection with the quadriceps–knee interdependence.)
5. Exercise 13 Thigh strengthener (p. 46). Slowly to begin with, speeding up if there is no pain. Follow the instructions on page 47 for fuller details of progression. (This, too, is an exercise concerned with the quadriceps–knee relationship, but it also works the hamstring muscles on the back of the thigh.)
6. Exercise 14 Running on the spot (p. 48).
7. Exercise 25 Heel strike walking (p. 70).
8. Exercise 33 Cycling (p. 84).
9. Exercise 34 Alternate knee bends ('Superglue' exercise) (p. 86).
10. Exercise 26 Slow motion running (p. 72).

ADDITIONAL EXERCISES FOR KNEE PROBLEMS

1. Exercise 3 Sideways leg swinging (p. 26).
2. Exercise 4 Corkscrew (p. 28). If you do this so that the 'pivot' goes all the way down to your toes, this will put a rotational force through the knee, which is helpful for cartilage or ligament problems. But remember not to push through pain!
3. Exercise 35 Both legs bend and stretch (p. 88).
4. Exercise 10 Curl up and stretches (p. 40). This is very good for mobilising a stiff knee joint, but very hard work. *Not* for the senior citizen.
5. Exercise 11 Ankle rises (p. 42). This is specifically for the calf muscle, but the calf is very close to the knee.
6. Exercise 27 Backwards walking (p. 74).
7. Exercise 28 Sideways walking (p. 76).

8. Exercise 29 Braiding (p. 78). This is difficult both in terms of balance and also because, by twisting the knee, it stresses the ligaments.
9. Exercise 30 Free style walking (p. 79).
10. Exercise 31 Running (p. 80).
11. Exercise 32 Resisted walking (p. 82).

FOOT AND ANKLE PAIN

Feet

If you have ever suffered from a pain in the foot or ankle, you will know how difficult it is not to develop a limp. Pain in the feet may happen because of many causes, and it is important to seek advice from an appropriate professional for any pain which is present for a time. The professional could be your doctor, a state registered chiropodist or state registered physiotherapist. It may be possible to cure the underlying cause of the problem, and that is obviously the best thing to do. In the play of life, every part of the body has an important role, but the feet are often treated as a mere 'walk-on' part. Their workings are taken for granted, and it is only when something goes wrong that one realises how important they are.

Probably the most common cause of pain in the feet is the result of wearing badly fitting footwear. This abuse may be recent, or it may have happened a long time ago, possibly even in childhood. In fact, feet are very complex structures. There are 26 bones in all and they are all supposed to move on one another.

Feet have evolved and the basic engineering is wonderful, but they were not designed for the wearing of shoes. I am not advocating that we should all burn our shoes, as the health hazards from not wearing shoes (at least in Western societies) are greater than from wearing them. However, I do think that the Oriental practice of removing shoes at home has a lot to recommend it. It allows for the feet to move in the way that nature intended and not be continuously encapsulated.

Almost everybody I know walks with 'kipper' feet. By this term I mean that the whole foot moves in one piece, pivoting from the heel. This is rather like holding a kipper by the tail and flapping it against the ground. This is the opposite, surely, of a springy walk which allows all the little joints to glide on each other, and which features the various parts of the feet.

When walking, there are three basic positions of the feet. (Fig. 7/3):

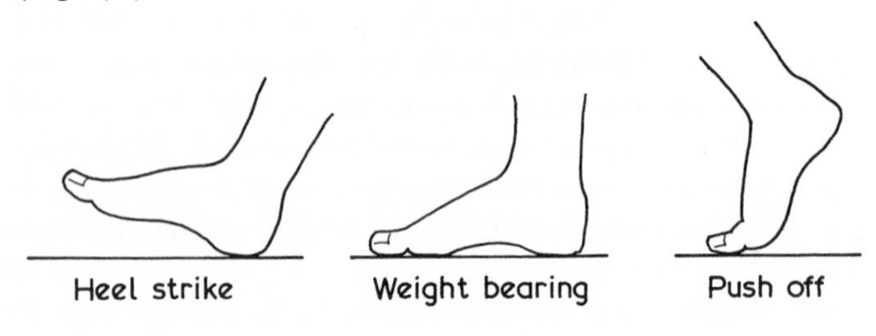

Fig. 7/3 Walking

Heel strike. As the foot hits the ground, the heel only should be in contact, and the rest of the foot should be held up.

Weight-bearing. The whole foot should be flat, so that there is maximum area for the weight to go through, but the two important arches in the foot (the longitudinal arch and the more important transverse arch) should be tightened up.

Push off. Finally, as the body-weight is being carried foward on to the other leg, some of that forward propulsion should come from the muscles in the big toe pushing against the ground, so that the back of the foot is raised, and the whole foot is in a 'tip-toe' position.

It is the last stage which often gets forgotten, and though it is perfectly feasible to practise this on dry land, it is very much easier in the water, as there is no weight going through the foot. This makes it a lot easier for the muscles and may well remove any pain.

Ankle

The spraining of an ankle is a very common complaint, and unfortunately can often recur. Sprained ankles recover quickly if they are treated early by physiotherapy, possibly ice packs and ultrasound. Once a sprain has happened, then all the muscles around the ankle can go into a state of shock and the normal sensory co-ordination is upset. An ankle is not fully recovered until you are able to stand on one leg (the one with the injured ankle) for at least 2 minutes, without holding on to anything. Exercises in water can help this even in the early stages, but care has to be taken. The water should be shoulder high, so that no weight is going through the ankle, and all movements should be done very gently to begin with.

Suggested exercises for foot and ankle problems

1. Exercise 1 Changes (p. 22).
2. Exercise 9 One-legged ankle rolls (p. 38).
3. Exercise 11 Ankle rises (p. 42).
4. Exercise 12 Knee bends (p. 44).
5. Exercise 13 Thigh strengthener (p. 46).
6. Exercise 14 Running on the spot (p. 48).
7. Exercise 25 Heel strike walking (p. 70). The more the better.

8. Exercise 26 Slow motion running (p. 72).
9. Exercise 27 Backwards walking (p. 74).
10. Exercise 28 Sideways walking (p. 76).
11. Exercise 29 Braiding (p. 78).
12. Exercise 30 Free-style walking (p. 79).
13. Exercise 31 Running (p. 80).
14. Exercise 32 Resisted walking (p. 82).

SHOULDER AND ARM PAIN

Quite a number of patients I see, who come to me because they are suffering from pain in the shoulder or down the arm, are not candidates for Aquarobics, at least not until the later recovery stages. Pain that is felt in the shoulder or arm may be caused by a lesion in the neck, the chest, or even the heart. Even if one knows that the pain is coming from a musculo-skeletal source, it is still very difficult to diagnose between the neck, the joints in the shoulder area, or any of the many muscles and tendons in the area. Indeed, in my experience, the cause of pain is very often a combination of the above alternatives. Check with your doctor before starting Aquarobics.

If your pain is diagnosed as coming from your neck, then these exercises will probably not help you. They may even make you worse. While on the subject, breast-stroke swimming is bad for neck problems. It is much better to swim on your back than on your front.

There are some local inflammatory conditions around the shoulder which can be extremely painful. An acute or irritable joint is one which is inflamed to such an extent that the slightest movement brings on a lot of pain, which then takes minutes to subside. A chronic joint problem, on the other hand, is one where a lot of provocation brings on pain, but the pain is not so severe and it stops as soon as the provocation ceases. Aquarobics is not suitable for acute shoulder problems, but it may help the chronic or subsiding conditions, providing one observes the 'do not push through pain' principle.

Shoulder and arm Aquarobics must be performed in shoulder-high water. If the pool is too shallow, then bend your knees so that the tip of your shoulders is just at water level. On dry land, the mechanics of lifting the arm out to the side are extremely complicated and involve many muscles working in a co-ordinated way. This is usually the first movement to suffer if there is a problem in the area. However, in water, the arm simply floats up to shoulder height without any muscle work. In fact it is the opposite of the situation on dry land – the muscles have to work to push the arm down.

I have had a few patients in the pool who have incidentally happened to have a swollen arm as a result of an earlier mastectomy operation (removal of a breast). The reason for taking part in an Aquarobic class has been unrelated to their swollen arm. However, I have observed in all cases that the swelling became reduced and softened after doing strong arm exercises in water. Even just 'marching' in the water was helpful. Probably it was just the pressure of the water combined with the pump action of muscles which reduced the swelling.

It is a good idea to work the muscles of the shoulder girdle before actually getting on to the arm muscles themselves, but I still think that Exercise 1 Changes, is the best exercise with which to start. In addition to the exercises listed below, swimming is certainly an appropriate exercise for the arms and shoulders, but I believe that swimming is only for later stages and that the specific exercises will bring about a more rapid recovery than just swimming as the only activity.

Suggested exercises for shoulder and arm problems

1. Exercise 1 Changes (p. 22).
2. Exercise 16 Shoulder shrugging (p. 52).
3. Exercise 17 Elbow cycling (p. 54).
4. Exercise 18 Shoulder girdle bend and stretch (p. 56).
5. Exercise 19 Elbow bends (p. 58).
6. Exercise 20 Passing round and under (p. 60).
7. Exercise 21 Arm swinging (p. 62).
8. Exercise 22 Cutting a diamond (p. 64).
9. Exercise 23 Arm walking (p. 66).
10. Exercise 24 Arm action for breast stroke (p. 68).
11. Exercise 26 Slow motion running (p. 72).
12. Exercise 32 Resisted walking (p. 82).

8
Aquarobics and Age

CHILDREN

I have gone through an Aquarobic routine with a few children whose legs have just come out of plaster of Paris, following fractures of the legs. The system does work, but may not be sufficiently stimulating for a lively youngster, and so might need 'pepping up'. Obviously the child has to be tall enough to be able to walk in the water, which might present a problem in a deeper pool. It is also helpful if the child can swim, or at least is not frightened of the water. The two things tend to go together in my experience.

Once or twice I have been able to have two children together, and this is much better as it brings in the competitive element. If you are the parent of a child who has just come out of plaster, and who is allowed to take weight through the bad leg, then try some initially gentle Aquarobics. *But*, check first with your medical adviser.

Aquarobics are probably quite helpful for asthmatic children, but follow the guidance given in the preceding chapters and in the paragraph above.

UNDER 40

In this age-group it is much more likely, statistically speaking, that you will be doing the exercises for 'keep-fit', rather than 'get-fit' reasons. There are no special warnings to issue other than those indicated in the previous chapters. Do please remember the principles, especially the 'moderation and sensible progression' one.

AGED 40 TO 60

This tends to be the dangerous age, when one does not know one's limitations. If you are accustomed to doing exercise, then there should be no problem. If, however, you are moved to immersion by this book – then do proceed cautiously and sensibly. Remember, particularly, the 'do not push through pain' principle.

Osteopurosis (or thinning of the bones) is a condition which usually affects women after the change of life. There is good reason to believe that exercising in water is helpful.

OVER 60

Do please get your doctor's approval before starting. If you are beginning to feel the tiredness that comes from old age, then do proceed much more cautiously than usual. Remember to allow enough energy to cope with the hassle of retrieving your clothes and getting dressed afterwards. Do try and rest at the pool before you leave, especially if the weather is cold. When you get home, allow time to go and lie down for a little while. This is really just a question of common sense.

9

Aquarobics Before and After Childbirth

The way in which an expectant mother's body adapts during pregnancy is another of nature's wonders. Changes begin in very early pregnancy to prepare for the 'packaging' of another person within the same framework. Quite early on, special hormones alter the structure of ligaments. This permits them to be stretched to make space for the growth of the baby. At the same time many other changes are happening, all of which should help put the 'mum' in peak physical fitness. But exercise helps, too, and Aquarobics are a useful way of exercising weightlessly, right up to and shortly after the birth. At all times remember the principle of 'moderation and sensible progression'. However, there are a few special precautions to note during the latter half of pregnancy and for the first few weeks after birth. (During early pregnancy no specific precautions are necessary, although, of course, the usual principles and warnings still apply.)

The altered shape of later pregnancy is achieved by the stretching and parting of some of the abdominal muscles. This inevitably weakens them. It is therefore essential that any exercise that works the abdominals should be done gently, while they are in that weakened state. The two long vertical muscles (the recti abdominis) that usually are joined together in the mid-line slide apart to accommodate the 'bulge'. They should meet together again a few days after the baby is born. Any exercise that is done while they are still apart should *not* pull them further apart. This means that if

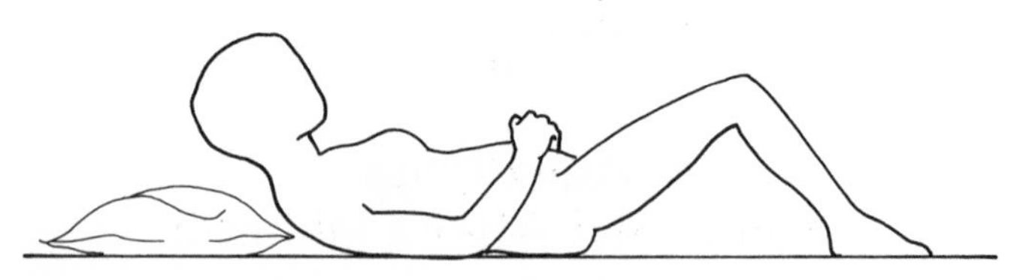

Fig. 9/1 How to feel if there is a gap in the recti abdominis (abdominal) muscles

the recti muscles are apart, only the gentlest of abdominal exercises should be done.

The way to test whether the recti abdominis muscles are still apart is to lie on your back on the floor or bed, with a pillow under your head, and with the knees bent up so that the feet are on the floor. Put one hand on your abdomen, and lift your head, breathing out as you do this (Fig. 9/1). You will feel the muscles tightening like two long vertical strands. However, if there is a soft gap in the middle which is wider than the width of one finger, your muscles have not yet come together, and very gentle exercise is the rule for the day. Some people believe that when you lift your head, if you cross your hands on your abdomen and gently push the muscles together, that this will encourage the gap to go more quickly.

It is better to err on the side of caution, and I would therefore suggest that Exercise 35 Both legs bend and stretch (p. 88) should be performed, allowing the big toes to get wet, thus taking the strain off the recti muscles.

POSTURE IN PREGNANCY (Fig. 9/2)

The additional bulge on the front of the abdomen (the baby) has the effect of increasing the normal curve (lordosis) in the small of the back. Often this gets extremely exaggerated and can cause back pain, or even sciatica. The way to correct this

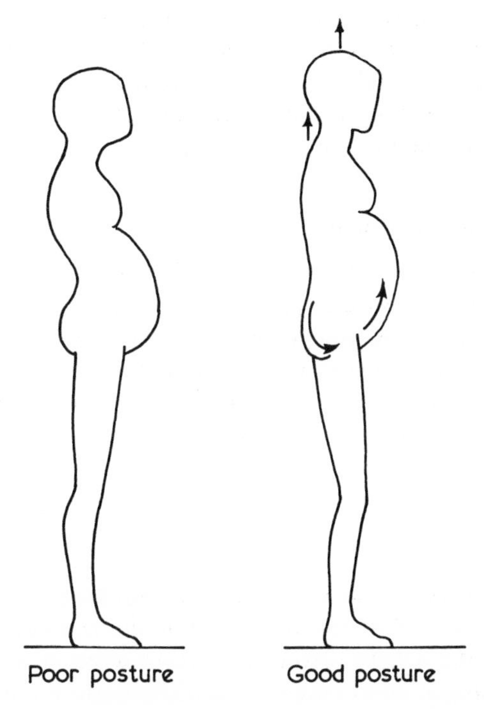

Fig. 9/2 Posture in pregnancy

is to try and flatten out the curve. You do this by lying on the floor, with the knees bent up so that the feet are on the floor, and then tighten the muscles of the abdomen and buttock so as to tilt the pelvis thus flattening the curve. When standing, try to repeat the same movement. Make yourself as tall as possible, keeping the chin tucked in, without forcing back the knees. It not only looks better, but it minimises strain on the back and helps prevent back pain.

Any exercise that swings the leg behind the body would tend to increase that lumbar curve. Therefore, Exercise 2 (p. 24) should only be done swinging the leg in front of the body in the later stages of pregnancy. After the baby is born it is all right to swing the leg behind you, but do make sure that you are pulling your abdomen in so that your back is flat. This can be checked by putting your spare hand on your hip bone and making sure that it remains stationary.

After a caesarean delivery

You must check with your doctor as to how soon you can do Aquarobics following a caesarean delivery. I have had people in the pool 10 days after giving birth by caesarean section with no problems. However, it is important to observe the 'do not push through pain' principle. The guidance given above relating to the recti muscles is equally true whichever way the baby was born.

Pelvic floor exercises

Regaining the normal use of the muscles of the perineum (or pelvic floor) is the most important of all the exercises to do after having a baby. Every new mum wants to regain her former shape, and hence has an incentive to do abdominal exercises. The pelvic floor cannot be seen, but if it is not functioning properly then stress incontinence can result. Also, slack pelvic floor muscles hinder good sex.

The pool has no particular role to play in re-educating the muscles of the pelvic floor. These tightening exercises can be done when 'spending a penny' (try to stop the flow), but certainly not to be done in this form in the pool.

Suggested exercises before and after having a baby

1. Exercise 1 Changes (p. 22).
2. Exercise 3 Sideways leg swinging (p. 26).

3. Exercise 4 Corkscrew (p. 28).
4. Exercise 7 Bumps and grinds (p. 34).
5. Exercise 8 Hula hoop (p. 36).
6. Exercise 11 Ankle rises (p. 42).
7. Exercise 12 Knee bends (p. 44).
8. Exercise 16 Shoulder shrugging (p. 52).
9. Exercise 26 Slow-motion running (p. 72).
10. Exercise 29 Braiding (p. 78).
11. Exercise 31 Running (p. 80).
12. Exercise 33 Cycling (p. 84).

10

Aquarobics for some Sports Injuries

Entire textbooks have been written on the subject of sports injuries and it is beyond the scope of this book to go into detail. It is important with sports injuries (as indeed it is important for all pains), to have a proper diagnosis. Once that has been given by an appropriate professional, and approval has been given for hydrotherapy, then proceed with suitable Aquarobic exercise, but taking note of the principles and the warnings.

I have observed when treating sportsmen that they tend to overdo their therapy. They have a mistaken belief that if they are told to do an exercise 50 times, it must do twice as much good if they do it 100 times – and they might as well increase the weights while they are at it. This is rubbish and is totally at loggerheads with the 'moderation and sensible progression' principle.

MUSCLE STRAINS

If a muscle has been strained (i.e. a few fibres pulled) then there are certain activities which I believe facilitate the rehabilitation process. They are in this order:

1. To work, i.e. contract, the muscle very gently so as to increase the blood supply in the injured muscle, which then speeds up the healing process.
2. Then to stretch gently the relaxed injured muscle (without

bouncing) so as to make sure that when it mends, it is not shortened by scar tissue.
3. Then to work the injured muscle more strongly, but *never pushing through pain*. (See Chapter 2.)

The three most commonly pulled muscles that I come across are the hamstrings (back of thighs), the quadriceps (front of thighs) and the gastrocnemius calf muscle. There is already sufficient guidance given in this book for the initial stages of sports rehabilitation, but it may be helpful to suggest ways to get the final fitness back in an athletic leg muscle.

1. Go through all the exercises in the section on knees, but perform them quickly and strongly to fast, lively music.
2. Do as many of the exercises as are feasible wearing flippers. This is especially useful for the walking exercises.
3. Swim, using only the legs. The easiest way to do this is, when swimming on your front, to hold on to a float with both arms and kick with only your legs. Alternately lie on your back and swim only with your legs, but use your arms to help to stabilise you.
4. For a *calf muscle* injury, it is always difficult at first to get the heel down. A good way to work the calf muscle is Exercise 11 Ankle rises (p. 42). As the muscle approaches full fitness, it will be possible to do the hard version of this, standing in shallower water on just the bad leg.
5. An inflated armband, or inner tyre tube placed under the foot is a strong resistance against which the *quadriceps* and *hamstring* muscles can work. Stand with the tyre under your bad foot (Fig. 10/1) and allow the heel of that leg to slide up the inside of the other shin. You will have to work hard to prevent the inflatable 'shooting' up to the surface.

Fig. 10/1 A strong exercise for thigh mucles – pushing down a tyre

When the knee is bent to a right angle, while facing in front of you, then push the foot straight down against the resistance of the tyre, so that both legs are again straight and together.

Index